MW00935380

Magic of Intention

Know Your Intention, Design Your Future

By
Karin Janin

Bloomington, IN  Milton Keynes, UK

authorHOUSE®

AuthorHouse™
1663 Liberty Drive, Suite 200
Bloomington, IN 47403
www.authorhouse.com
Phone: 1-800-839-8640

AuthorHouse™ UK Ltd.
500 Avebury Boulevard
Central Milton Keynes, MK9 2BE
www.authorhouse.co.uk
Phone: 08001974150

First published by AuthorHouse 2/22/2007

ISBN: 1-4184-9081-4 (sc)

Library of Congress Control Number: 2004096224

Printed in the United States of America
Bloomington, Indiana

This book is printed on acid-free paper.

www.magicofintention.com

DEDICATED TO

This book is dedicated to my husband, Sherm.

His continued support, love and patience has carried me through

the creation of this book.

TABLE OF CONTENTS

ACKNOWLEDGEMENTS

My heartfelt thanks go to many, many people who have believed in this project.

Thanks to Perry A~ Speaker and Author: and friend who insisted on being on the review list and let me know often that what I have written is something others will want to read.

Thanks to Lori Bonfitto, Screenplay Writer: who has been my angel cheerleader and believed in my project more than I did from the beginning.

Thanks to Larry Czerwonka, Creative Genius, whom I have never met but who believed in me years ago when I first started *The Orphan Connection*. He has been a shinning light behind all my goals.

Thanks to Ellen Chase, Teacher, Entrepreneur: who has believed in me all the way.

Thanks to Ines De Toro, Life Coach, friend and Spanish Translator in Bogotá, Columbia: who has been a wonderful support and good friend.

Thanks to Dr. Stan Friedland, Educator, Author for his wonderful sense of humor and words of encouragement.

Thanks to RoxAnne Franklin, Professional Photographer and Journalist: who made me laugh at all the silly things that happened along this journey.

My thanks to Roger King, Author and Speaker: who took the time out of his busy speaking schedule and writing projects to review my material and send magical words of encouragement.

Thanks to Chelle Thompson, Editor and founder of Inspiration Line: for spending and many hours editing my material, making suggestions and encouraging me all the way.

Thanks to Dee Saunders, Instructor-Expressive Arts Therapy: whose patience and encouragement have helped me along this writing journey.

Thanks to Gay Smith, Free Lance Editor/Proof Reader: who made sure that my thoughts and personality were not lost in the "translation."

Thanks to Lee Sprengel, Writer: whose funny stories have kept me laughing during the most trying times.

Thanks to Joanne Susi, Mentor Coach and Teacher: who taught me all that I know about intentions. She cared, she laughed, she applauded.

FORWARD

In this wonderful book, Karin gives us practical guidelines on how to manage change in our lives. She concentrates on you, the reader, and helps you find the Magic that is in everyone of us.

I have known Karin for nearly two years and as I read her book I felt the magical intention of her book inspire my soul. It is a book that you can pick up and read anywhere.

The "Magic of Intention" will get you back on track and feed your mind, heart and soul, with "gently thought provoking food." It will help you grow and feel safe through your journey of change.

This book has the knack of being easy to read and will open your mind to going within yourself to find YOUR "magic!"

She is an empowered woman with an inspiring story and a lot of every day common sense. She lives what she writes without preaching! Karin is my friend and mentor

Keep this book close by, perhaps in your handbag or by your bedside. You will not regret one minute spent on the exercises, meditations, and visualizations which are included.

Have fun reading the "Magic of Intention!"

~ Roger King, *SoulTalkStories.com*

.....work like you don't need money,

Love like you've never been hurt,

And dance like no one's watching!

~ Author Unknown

Are you ready to go from...............

......ordinary to extraordinary?

......jobless to employed?

......disconnected to connected?

......confusion to confidence?

......chaos to order and peace?

......blocked to open and free?

I dedicate the Magic found in this book

to YOU and a better life NOW!

INTRODUCTION

Let the magic begin!

Magic!

Magic. What a powerful word! When I think of Magic, I think of Merlin…a magical person in a magical time. Sure, some of today's magic is an illusion. But, the Magic we will be talking about in this book is not an illusion…it is real and reachable.

---

*"Everyday affirms the **magic** of the Universe and the miracles that can happen through the power of intention."*

~ Chelle Thompson,

InspirationLine.com

Intentions are magical. As Chelle says, "Miracles can happen through the power of Intention." It just takes a little effort on your part to stir up the magic.

This book is full of powerful, Magical information which brings the Wizard of Change into your life to create the positive future YOU desire now! Initially I will discuss background information about intentions, how our mind is manipulated in positive or negative ways, how we must learn to reprogram our subconscious mind which contains imprints that hinder our progress, plus so much more. Finally, it will be your turn to create your own intentions. There will be pages of sample of intentions from A-Z. Included will be spaces for you to write your own intentions.

Just imagine that you are beginning a new journey, one that will be filled with change and choices. As on any journey, tools will be necessary on this magical path that you have chosen to take: A compass for direction, lots of emotional support, a scattering of magical thoughts, a willingness for change to happen, and the ability to perceive a future which is happening NOW!

Are you ready to take the next step? Are you ready to take the wand of words, grab the magical hat, put the "old you" inside the hat and see the "new you" flying out? Feel the positive changes in your life happening NOW.

The Wizard within comes forward – let the Magic begin NOW!

My journey into intentions

I remember, years ago being asked to state an "intention." At that time I did not have a clue as to what someone meant by that so I dismissed it. The word intention felt like something that was intangible and elusive.

As time went on, I would join different groups – support, meditation, and others – and again and again the word "intention" popped up. So I decided to learn about this subject. I began to research what others had written as I knew this concept was not new.

I learned that the idea of intention had been around for centuries. In fact, Aristotle often spoke of man's intention. He used the Greek word "proaireton" which is a compound verb that means "to choose before." What Aristotle was talking about are the choices in life that we make before we take action.

In my exploration I had a wonderful mentor/coaching intrustructor by the name of Joanne Susi, who taught me how to write an intention. Joanne is one of those people that you meet once in a great while….she is knowledgeable, funny, caring, patient and insightful. Through her direction I learned how to write or say an intention. Once I "got it" my life began changing for the better almost immediately.

"Man's word is his wand filled with magic and power!"

~ Florence Scovel Shinn,

Spirituality Writer

I have been told many times that all you need to do is just say or think an intention.

They say *technique does not matter...* but that is not completely true.

"When one door of happiness closes, another opens; but often we look so long at the closed door that we do not see the one which has opened for us. "

~ Helen Keller

Author, Activist for the Blind

The technique that I will be introducing to you will make sense once you have learned it and tried it out a couple of times.

It is designed to give you direct access to your subconscious mind.

This will be discussed more in Chapter 2.

As I began understanding what an intention is and how it has made a great difference in my life, it became easier and easier for me to write one. Eventually I started writing or saying more than one a day and my life changed for the better..

As with any journey, I quickly realized how important it was for me to look inside and discover who I am, what I really want, and what it would take to get to a place of success in all areas of my life.

The good news is that I can write or say an intention quickly and easily now. I find hopes and dreams begin to happen quickly because I have learned to be in alignment with my belief system, I am clear about my intention, and I know that "this will happen."

I trust the invisible intention to manifest.

"Minds, like parachutes, function better when open"

~ Peter Shepherd

Transformational Psychologist

My wish for you is that you experience the Magic quickly and effortlessly once you understand the mechanics of an intention.

Join me on this journey and be open to the MAGIC that is within you.

The following page is a contract to YOURSELF which you can fill out, make a copy and place within visual reach to be reminded of it from time to time.

Once you have signed the contract and made a copy, you can then move onto the next page and prepare for the Magic to happen by reading the meditations and writing your experiences.

Most exercises, meditations, and visualizations, will include my experiences for you to read as an example.

SIGN IT - MAKE A COPY- FRAME IT OR PUT IT

SOMEWHERE SO YOU CAN SEE IT OFTEN.

I _____*(name)*

am ready to embrace the

MAGIC OF INTENTION

and move forward with my life.

I agree to work on positive Magical Intentions that will make a

difference in my life and possibly the lives of others.

I agree to be

Clear

In Alignment with my highest good

To get excited

To trust the Infinite Intelligence

from this day _____*forward.*

I _____*(name)*

say

YES to a brighter future NOW!

Meditation: Preparing for the Magic

The following is a short meditation to prepare you for The Magic to begin. If you would like, put some soft music on, light a candle, burn some incense. Create a meditative space that works for you.

Close your eyes when you are ready.

Just relax and breathe in and out slowly- breathing in love, breathing out anger, doubt, frustration, fear or whatever is troubling you.

Imagine your body is relaxing even more from the top of your head to the bottom of your feet... just relaxing more and more.

Now imagine that you are surrounded with beautiful, colored stars. They are twinkling brightly above you.

You feel safe and comfortable with them.

Imagine you are opening up to your Infinite Intelligence. As you are opening up, the stars start to move down towards you like Magic. Swirling gently all around you as if creating a blanket of safety and security.

Just bathe in the beauty of the moment.

When you are ready, slowly open your eyes, feeling rested... filled with wonderment and excitement. How do you feel? Write your experience on the next page.

Meditation: Preparing for the Magic – (Write your experience here)

Meditation: Preparing for the Magic *(Sharing my experience)*

This is one of my favorite meditations. It is short and reminds me how essential it is to breathe in and out and RELAX... something I tend to forget to do with my very busy schedule. As a certified instructor of hypnosis and a life coach, I have few problems helping my clients relax. Yet when it comes to myself, I need a little reminding. This quick meditation is the right "prescription" for me.

My experience: Oh, the beautiful stars... at night. I love to see the twinkling of stars. It is easy for me to imagine the stars above me. I felt very safe and protected while journeying into the meditations. My first impressions were comfort, safety and beauty. When I felt the stars "swirling gently all around me as if creating a blanket of safety and security," I felt a strong sense of peace come over me and that I was truly in touch with the Infinite Intelligence. How blessed I am – the sense of gratitude is strong. What a beautiful moment – a moment I can take with me wherever I go.

Did you write your experience?

Know that everyone's experience
will be different because we are all Magically Unique!

PART I

GROUND WORK

ROOTS OF INTENTION

Chapter 1

Life starts with intention.

An intention is a statement with purpose. Each time we shake our head, touch our toes, get up, sit down, we are doing it with intention.

----

*"A gift consists not in what is done or given, but in the **intention** of the giver or doer."*

Lucius Annaeus Seneca

Roman Playwright (3 BC-65 AD)

Every animal, plant and human being started with intention. We are born with intention – we are not separate from it.

Some call it an "energy field that cannot be explained. "

The foundation of our existence was created by intention.

Our thoughts, actions, and words are <u>creative</u> intentions. Everything including amoebas, cells insects, plants and humans, live with intention. Take a minute and think about prehistoric time. Intention was focused on survival then. All animals, plants, and man created ways to survive the austerity of the land. Yes, some species no longer exist, but life on this planet with all its intention, continues.

By now you are probably thinking, I'm stretching it a little – but if you look around your environment, every creature has intent, every cell in our body functions with intent to work in unison with other parts of our body.

As humans we rationalize everything – that is why it takes us so long to figure out the simple things that other creatures have known all along. When we are born, we enter a life full of intentions – to be happy, to be content, to giggle and wiggle, to crawl, walk, be loved, grow, have a family, live a full life, and make a peaceful transition. ***But what about…..***

What about the people who are abused, starving, disabled, homeless, constantly experiencing war, famine, catastrophes? What is their intention? Where is the Magic in their lives?

3

There is such a thing as the Ying and the Yang of intention. Sciencetology calls the negative intention a "counter intention." If you intend to spend your life angry, your life will attract angry people and situations. If you intend to spend your life starving, then you will attract starvation. If you have the attitude that "this is my lot in life," then that is what you will attract.

I know there are, for example, disabled individuals who spend their lives not being angry, but accepting their situation and being a positive example for other disabled people. Heather Mills McCartney is an example of this. She lost her leg to a freak accident, and now she works to see to it that everyone who has lost a leg can receive a leg replacement. Her charity is called the *Heather Mills McCartney Cosmesis*. Her intentions are positive. She is giving "life" and a brighter future for those who have experienced this type of loss.

People who have experienced horrific things in their lives, may not understand the Power and Magic of Intentions. They may also be shut down due to depression or other factors. There are a lot of situations that we, as humans, can change and will be able to change.

Through better understanding and spreading the word about positive change, we are not only helping ourselves, we are helping others.

My journey:

My journey in this lifetime started off as an orphan in Germany at the close of the last World War. I lived there for the first four years of my life. Where was my Magic then?

I am sure I kept the Magic of intention stirred within my heart and soul, but due to the unpleasant environment I lived in, I was unable to see or feel beyond my own emotional pain. But, silently, the Magic was stirring within me through a strong desire to be loved and to love. Eventually I was "found" and transported to Caracas, Venezuela, by a wealthy philanthropist.

Later, I was adopted by an American family. Then tragedy occurred and my adopted father, whom I loved dearly, died of a heart attack. Where was the Magic of intention in that? Intention does not just disappear. Sometimes we block out the good that comes from unfortunate events due to our sorrow. That is what I did for a long time.

I was young and did not understand what was happening. Years later, I realized that I had been given the greatest gift of all which is unconditional love. I wanted and intended to be loved and I received it! How blessed I was.

I have had a series of ups and downs in my life, but the Magic never left me. I was the one that shut down from time to time due to the events in my life. But the Magic, never, ever left me. And it will never, ever leave you!

As you read this book you will come to understand what intention is, how it can work for you, what steps are needed to make it work, and how your intentions influence others. Meditations and writing exercises will be included throughout this book to help you become clearer in what it is you really want out of your life.

You are what your deepest desire is
As your desire, so is your intention.
As is your intention, so is your will.
As is your will, so is your deed.
As is your deed, so is your destiny.

~ The Ancient Vedic

<u>Our</u> desire is our destiny.

What we think (intention – desire) is our destiny. For this reason, we must be <u>clear</u> about what Intention is and how to write or say a statement of intention that is in our best interest.

How many times have we said things like: "I will get organized, I will change my life, I will lose weight, I will do this and that." We all have good intentions, but what happens to those good intentions?

So much of the time we do not believe in our inherent goodness and in our abilities to follow through. It is our lack of self-confidence that holds us back. This has been my issue for years and in retrospect, I can see how I, and I alone, kept myself from succeeding. Since I have been working with intentions, my life has truly changed and so will yours.

All I ask from you is that you be open to the possibilities that Magical Intentions will change your life for the good. Below is a meditation entitled "Soaring to the heights of success." It is a short meditation. Once you are through, be sure to immediately go to the next page and write your impressions.

Most exercises, meditations, and visualizations,

will include my experiences for you to read as an example.

Remember, we are not alike and your experience

will be different from mine.

Meditation: Soaring to heights of success

Before you start, create an environment that is safe, peaceful and relaxing. Put some music on, burn a candle, feel yourself going into relaxation NOW.

Breathe in and out slowly relaxing.

For a minute look out a window, any window. Make a mental picture of what you see.

Now, go beyond what you are seeing and imagine your spirit starting to soar.

Just allow your spirit to soar and be free to seek what you most want to achieve.

What is it you want achieve?

7

Get in touch with your emotions.

How does that feel?

Take a mental picture of what you are "seeing" and "feeling"
and bring it back into the room where you are.

———————————————

Record your experience below.

Date it and store it in a safe place.

——————

Most exercises, meditations, and visualizations,

will include my experiences for you to read as an example.

Remember, we are not alike and your experience

will be different from mine.

Meditation (Spirit Soaring): *(Write your experience here)*

Meditation (Spirit Soaring): *(Sharing my experience)*

There is nothing I love more than to pretend I am soaring, flying through the sky like a bird. Carefree. A sense of freedom overwhelms me and I feel that I can do ANYTHING I make up my mind to do. While soaring I felt myself filled with a great sense of personal worth.

I am receiving applause

I have a" Can Do" attitude

Attitude/Gratitude/Happiness/Joy

I am Proud

I clearly see myself speaking in front of a large group. No longer a fearful experience, but a warm one. I am greeted with a loud, thundering applause and all learn from me as I learn from them.

When I am ready to be grounded (land with both feet on the ground) I do so softly and with intent.

And at anytime I wish to soar, I can because

I KNOW I CAN!

Thank you of wonderful Infinite Wisdom.

This is my day.

There will be more wonderful days like this.

CONSCIOUS, SUBCONSCIOUS, AND SUPERCONSCIOUS "MINDS"

Chapter 2

We have a great mind with an endless potential. That potential is developed with the assistance of the conscious, subconscious and superconscious parts of our mind.

We often refer to these parts as *separate minds*.

Our goal is to have all these parts working together as One Mind.

While discussing the different parts of our mind, we will also look at the Critical Factor which may be holding us back from our full potential.

Our conscious "mind" is our awake state. It is the part that makes instant decisions on what the whole person perceives to be their truth.

----

*"The **conscious mind** is self-knowing, self-assertive, it has will, choice and may accept or reject. It is the only part of our mind that can think independently of circumstances."*

~ **Roger King,** *Motivational Speaker, Author,*

As Roger observes, the conscious "mind" is independent and can accept or reject what it has "seen, heard, or felt." The problem is our conscious "mind" is also our Ego state and it generally wants to be right. It is a part of our drive and there is nothing wrong with having a good healthy Ego. In fact, many of us should work on it – including myself!

The trouble with each impression that the conscious "mind" receives, be it positive or negative, is that those impressions are registered in the subconscious "mind" and thus imprinted into our human computer.

We receive conscious impressions through the media, through early childhood, through our peers, through our self-talk, and in dozens of other ways. Some impressions are better than others.

For example, we have all seen the results of violent media impressions.

----

*"There is a principle called the Law of Expression, which says that whatever is expressed is **impressed**. This means that whatever you say, whatever you express to another in your conversation, is impressed into your **subconscious mind**. Everything that you think, imagine, say, do or feel triggers everything else, like a chain reaction."*

~ ***Brian Tracy***,

Author – 'Million Dollar Habits'

For example: I have often used the phrase, "I am stupid." My subconscious "mind" will simply believe it when regularly repeated. So the next time I say "I am not stupid" my subconscious "mind" will check its "data base" and reject what I have just said. The feeling of "being stupid" prevails until I make some serious changes in the use of the negative word combinations.

How many times have you lost your keys? I know I have more than once! In my rushing around and becoming frustrated, I have found myself saying, "I am losing my mind, can't find my keys" Of course, I am really not losing my mind, I only misplaced my keys. But, the subconscious still believes what I have said about my mind. In other words, it believes what I have just said. The statement becomes a fact. And until I stop saying that "I am losing my mind" or replace that thought with positive words like the "keys are within reach" or "I will find the keys in just a moment" the subconscious is just going to keep reminding me what I have programmed into it.

I do <u>not</u> want to lose my mind so I am making a conscious effort to watch my thoughts and words. Yes, thoughts are unspoken words and can do as much damage as the spoken word. By the way, I always do find my keys.

---

*"The **subconscious mind** produces best what you dwell on. That's why you especially end up experiencing exactly what you worry about."*

~ **Sonia Choquette**, **Ph.D.**, *Author, Speaker, Psychic*

<u>Words are powerful.</u>

They can heal or destroy,

can bring depression or joy,

can bring success or failure.

Be aware of what goes into the subconscious "mind."

We as humans naturally say things off the top of our head. We cannot feel guilty every time we say something negative, but awareness of your words is another key to your Magic. Just notice what you have said, and with practice you will have more positive programming than negative going into your subconscious "mind."

Bypassing the Critical Factor

You may be asking what I mean by the Critical Factor. It is the "thing" that determines the success of any project. All businesses look at the Critical Factors that will ultimately lead to success or failure of a project. *For example,* NASA relies heavily on deciphering the "critical factor" which could hinder a space program's success.

This same concept holds true not only in our outside world, but within each of us.

Let's have some fun and give the Critical Factor a name. It will be called the "Sneaky Little Computer Virus." (**SLCV**) Now, just imagine this is a **SLCV** found between the conscious and the subconscious "mind." This little virus is the naysayer or the "devils advocate." The chatter that says "you can't change, you can't do this or that" and every time you want to reprogram, the **SLCV** shows up, standing guard. While the conscious "mind" is analytical, rational, and has access to will power, it can be undermined by subconscious thoughts.

You desire to make changes and may wonder how that can happen. It can only happen through bypassing the **SLCV** (formerly known as the Critical Factor).

Once you disarm and unblock the Critical Factor, you then....

1) block negative thinking (**SLCV**) from passing into you subconscious "mind," and

2) allow change to happen.

How do you do that? The easiest way is through visualization. There is an old saying "Seeing is believing."

We will explore visualization more in Chapter 6.

Included in this chapter is an exercise which deals the Sneaky Little Computer Virus. You may write your experience in the space provided. Should you need more room, please provide yourself with additional paper. This is a crucial exercise in the progress of your potential and goals. Be honest with yourself as no one is judging you but you. There are no right or wrong answers so be honest with yourself.

———————

Most exercises, meditations, and visualizations,

will include my experiences for you to read as an example.

Remember, we are not alike and your experience

will be different from mine.

Exercise: Blocking and disarming **SLCV** *(aka the Critical Factor)*
(Write your experience-mine will follow yours)

Think about a time that you wanted to do something and that Sneaky Little Computer Virus stopped you from achieving your goal. What did SLCV say?

It's time to have a little talk with SLCV. Imagine yourself talking to it. Go back and forth with the conversation. This is between YOU and YOU, so be honest. Now write down your innermost feelings about this conversation and ask yourself "Who is in charge?"

Exercise: Blocking and disarming **SLCV** *(continued)*

Time to disarm SLCV.

Take your Magical wand and imagine that SLCV is being neutralized. The path for new, positive programming is happening NOW. You are feeling empowered and know that you will now reach your goal because SLCV no longer blocks the way. It is completely disarmed!

Exercise: (Sharing my experience.)

SLCV said:

You can't life coach other people. Who do you think you are? Who is going to listen to you?

My conversation with the SLCV is:

Ok, SLCV. You've had a lot of fun for too many years with me. Now it's time that you take a back seat and let me be the achiever. I've done my homework. Ha! I have had many successful clients say to me that I am doing things right. I am a certified life coach AND am working on my Ph.D. But that's not all it takes to be successful. I have what it takes and you are no longer going to have power over me.

I am disarming and blocking the SLCV by:

Visualizing that SLCV disintegrates to nothingness. I am visualizing my success now. I am visualizing workshops, books, motivational cards, and intention circles being developed now. I am visualizing travel, success, and my personal power back in my hands. And I visualize myself thanking the Infinite Intelligence for all my good. So, I disarm and block you from this day forward! Adios.

Now how do you feel?

F R E E!

Superconscious

Many people refer to this state as the Higher Self, the Infinite Wisdom, Infinite Intelligence, Intuition, God, Angels, or Spirit Guides.

The *superconscious* "mind" is where thoughts of inspiration come from. The "ah-ha" moments.

"….supercomputer that can enable you to solve any problem, overcome any obstacle and achieve any goal you can set for yourself."

*~ **Brian Tracy**,*

Author – 'Million Dollar Habits'

Problems are solved by opening ourselves up to the superconscious "mind." For example, while writing this book, I have been in a state of confusion as there is so much I want to cover. I was trying to decide what should come first, then next and so forth. One night I went to sleep exhausted thinking about my book. I woke up the next morning with a clear plan of action. This happened because I was open and receptive.

The superconscious "mind" is your friend, your mentor and your guide.

With the assistance of the superconscious "mind" your conscious "mind" will make changes and those changes will go directly into your subconscious "mind."

*"The real mystic who has spiritual realizations of **superconscious** experiences becomes extremely interested in his fellow beings as he finds the expression of God in them. A mystic feels the presence of God everywhere and so he takes a loving interest not only in human beings but also in other beings."*

~ Swami Akhilananda
Author-Hindu Psychology

When people are "in touch" with their superconscious mind, they often devote their lives to humanity. They inspire because they are inspired by those whom they are helping These people often have a strong sense of "mission" or dharma.

Our ultimate desire in life should be helping others but we must first be able to understand who we are, and why we are behaving the way we do. In other words, what drives us. Letting the "ghosts out of our closets" will help clear the path to your success. In connecting with the superconscious and our conscious minds, we can be all that we want to be and have the life we desire.

Next is a visualization between you and your superconscious "mind."

Most exercises, meditations, and visualizations,
will include my experiences for you to read as an example.
Remember, we are not alike and your experience
will be different from mine.

Visualization: This is chat with your Superconscious "Mind"

Once again, breathe in and out slowly. Think of something you desire – a goal you would like to reach. Hold that thought.

Now close your eyes and relax, relax, relax – gently relaxing more and more. Visualize your goal or desire. Now, go directly to your Superconscious "mind" and have a little chat. Ask questions like:

How can I achieve _____?

What is my first step?

What are my stumbling blocks?

Be open and "listen." Ask your superconscious to have a talk with your conscious and subconscious "minds" and let them know that changes are coming and they are happening NOW!

Wave the Magical wand around and around, swirling the Energy of Change.

As you are imagining, feel your emotions associated with the imaging.

Be with this for about five or ten minutes.

If you don't receive a message right away, that's fine, trust that you will.

It's time to come back to the present moment.

Exercise: Superconscious *(Write your experience)*

Exercise: **Superconscious** *(Sharing my experience)*

A goal I would like to reach is to complete the writing of this book by the agreed time – which is early June. Ok, now I'm going to relax even more…I am closing my eyes while typing so I can be open to the answers. There is a bridge and a lovely creek below, flowing gently. And on the other side of the bridge is my superconscious or, as I like to think of it, the Infinite Source. I walk over the bridge and am greeted warmly by the Infinite Source. My heart flutters with excitement. We sit down in a comfortable setting and the Q&A session begins. The answers come to me telepathically from the Infinite Source to my conscious mind which is relaxed right now. I ask "how can I achieve this goal?" The IS replies, "Trusting Self – Stay Focused." I then ask "What is the First Step?" Infinite Source replies "Make an appointment to write everyday." I ask "What are my stumbling blocks?" Infinite Source says "You." Gulp! We talk about change and I'm already feeling an energy shift. The Magic is strong and I feel it. The right words for my book are swirling around my head. It is time for me to leave.

I thank Infinite Source for the time spent. Infinite Source gives me a gift to be opened once I stand on the bridge that unites the two "minds" and thank the Infinite Source.

The gift is the Magic of persistence and focus.

INTENTION vs. AFFIRMATION

Chapter 3

To be honest, there is little difference – and yet there is a large difference. Read on and you will understand what I am saying.

Webster's Dictionary definitions:

Affirmation – A <u>positive statement</u> asserting that a goal which the speaker or thinker wishes to achieve is <u>already</u> happening

Intention – The <u>quality or state</u> of having a <u>purpose</u> in mind.

Thesaurus:

Affirmation – confirmation, pronouncement, a statement

Intention – meaning, purpose, aim, goal, aspiration

Below is a chart that contains key words.

Affirmation	Intention
• Confirmation	• Meaning
• Pronouncement	• Purpose
• Statement	• Goal
• Announcement	• Aspiration

As you can see, an Intention and an Affirmation compliment each other.

Differences:

Intentions - *Aspire*

Affirmations - *Declare*

_____

"**Affirmations** *are very powerful tools for transformation and self-empowerment.*"

~ **Daily Affirmations**,

www.YourDailyAffirmation.com/

Affirmations are very much like intentions. But in order to think or write an affirmation, *one must have an intention.* Once again, it all starts with intention.

Distractions, obstacles and unclear goals all contribute to your inability to achieve what you have a right to achieve. Clear intentions will bring change and create new experiences that move us to our destiny.

In this book, we will talk about how to change what is keeping you from success.

Our experiences are shaped by our intentions. And at the same time, our experiences change our intentions.

But, first, you must have the courage to change. And then be persistent for change to happen.

"As you go along your road in life, you will, if you aim high enough, also meet resistance...but no matter how tough the opposition may seem, have courage still – and persevere."

~ Madeleine Albright

64th U.S. Secretary of State

In the beginning of this book I asked you, the reader, to sign a contract agreeing to be ready for changes to happen.

Take a minute and look at that contract again.

How does the contract look now?

Is it in a place where you can see it often?

Does it encourage?

If not, change it to fit your needs.

Most exercises, meditations, and visualizations,

will include my experiences for you to read as an example.

Remember, we are not alike and your experience

will be different from mine.

Exercise: Preparing for serious work *(Write your experience)*

Are you ready to do some serious work?

____ Yes ____ No

If the answer is NO, then when will you be ready?

If the answer is YES, then feel the excitement within you that is stirring.

Get in touch with your inner child and imagine that the two of you are going through a tunnel.

How dark is the tunnel?

What do you see at the other end?

The ancients used hieroglyphics as a means of communicating messages. Do you see some messages on the walls? What are they?

Exercise: Preparing for serious work (Sharing my experience)
Are you ready to do some serious work?
__x__ Yes ____ No
I am ready NOW!

If the answer is YES, then feel the excitement within you that is stirring. What does it feel like?

I feel the sense of mystery and awe in the journey through the tunnel. Can't wait to get to the other side to see how life can be better for me.

I am in touch with my inner child and we're walking together through the tunnel. This feels like *I am not alone. I feel lighter and confident that, together, we will find answers. I have the support of my inner child.*

How dark is the tunnel? *It is dark, very dark, but I am not frightened as I am not alone. Of course, I am anxious to get to the other end.*

What do you see at the other end? *There really is light at the other end of this tunnel. It's much like a picture I took a few years ago. Amazing. Warm and inviting*

The ancients used hieroglyphics as a means of communicating messages. Do you see some messages on the walls that will help you? What are they?

The messages all say that I need to trust my inner source and share this trust with my inner child. To let go of fear of the unknown and find joy in life NOW. I see the following words: "There will be people whom you will meet on this journey who will help you stay focused because they too, believe in you. Go my friend, hurry to the end of the tunnel. You will find it is what you have wished it to be."

I am running as fast as I can. I am there. The light is bright, and the music is mystically beautiful. I believe this is my heaven, which is on Earth NOW! I imagine myself laughing with joy and know that everything will be it is meant to be. I have walked through the door of destiny.

"I took a deep breath and listened to the old brag of my heart. I am, I am, I am."

~ Sylvia Plath, *Author*

PART II

WORKINGS OF AN INTENTION

CLARITY

Chapter 4

How many times have you said "I want to do such and such to achieve this or that" and yet, not really been clear about what it is you want to achieve? How many times have you felt that you knew the direction you wanted to take in order to succeed, only to find that the plan was not clear enough?

This is a tough chapter to face, even for myself. In order to believe in ones goals or intentions, one needs to be CLEAR.

The Magical key to CLARITY is identifying what your values are. For example do you just want to make lots of money for the sake of having it or do you want the personal freedom that comes from creating abundance in your life?

Being clear about your values will help clarify how you see yourself in the present and the future.

I was divorced for 20 years. In those 20 years, I had a few significant relationships. But nothing seemed to work and I finally gave up. I realized that I needed to specifically identify my values in order to be clear about type of relationship I wanted and deserved. Even more crucial, I had to understand that the most important relationship was with myself, not with another person. I value trustworthiness, personal power, freedom, being connected and spirituality. I realized that these were the same values I wanted in a healthy relationship with someone else. Once I allowed CLARITY on board, my life changed. (I am a slow learner – stubborn at times. *Have to do it MY WAY!*)

Guess what? I met my present husband on a plane and he's absolutely great! He is my friend, my lover, my confidant and my supportive cheerleader.

Once I realized what my personal needs, values and my passion were I was able to attract a healthy relationship.

"Reappraise the past, reevaluate where we've been, clarify where we are, and predict or anticipate where we are headed."

~ Toni Cade Bambara

Noted writer, Editor and Teacher

Exercise: Values *(Write your combinations)*

The following is a list of sample values. See how those fit in your life. Which combinations work for you? What are your core values?

Passion	Humor	Service
Personal Power	Excellence	Spirituality
Recognition	Freedom of Choice	Honesty
Accomplishment	Adventurous	Risk Taking
Connectedness	Peacemaking	Joy
Beauty	Accomplishment	Free Spirit
Success	Productivity	Authenticity
Nurturing	Tradition	Love

Here's a sample combination: Service/Peacemaker/Recognition?
Then perhaps you should start your own non-profit organization.

Now it's your turn:

You can add to this list, take something off, then re-do your combinations whenever you think that you have made a shift. Nothing stays the same, and we, as humans are never the same. Sure, some characteristics may never change but who we are deep inside does change with time and wisdom.

In order to be clear about your goal, you must be clear about your values.

The following few pages are steps designed to help you become *clearer* about your goals now that you are *clearer* about your values.

I have provided room for your answers. Take your time. This is not a test. You may find yourself changing while working through the steps.

"Learn from the mistakes of others. You can't live long enough to make them all yourself."

~ Eleanor Roosevelt

Activist and Former First Lady

Most exercises, meditations, and visualizations,

will include my experiences for you to read as an example.

Remember, we are not alike and your experience

will be different from mine.

Exercise: CLARITY (Write your experiences)

Step 1:

Understand who YOU are. Assess your life. What are your attributes? Look at all the positive things you have done. Focus on your positive rather than your negative attributes. Now start listing.

Step 2:

Clear out the clutter! Not only in your personal environment but your inner self. Throw out the garbage that is in the way of your progress. List what you are throwing away and notice your emotional state.

Step 3:

What are you passionate about? Don't be influenced by what others think you are or should be passionate about. This is about YOU. Be very clear. You may come back and add to this list from time to time, but go ahead and get started.

Step 4:

Who or what drains your energy? This can include people who are not emotionally healthy for you and any addictive behavior patterns. You can make a choice once you've made the list, to allow or not allow these people or negative situations into your life. **You are free to choose.**

Step 5:

What risks are you willing to take? Can you step out of the box?

Step 6:

What gives you confidence?

———————

"Whatever you can do, or dream you can, begin it. Boldness has genius, power, and magic in it."

~ Goethe,

German Playwright

Step 7:

What have you always wanted to do or be? What is stopping you now? What are you willing to do?

Step 8:

What is the <u>one</u> action that would make your dream/goal a reality?

Exercise: Clarity *(Sharing my experience)*

Step 1: *Understand who YOU are*

My achievements are: mother of three successful children, second marriage, degreed, published, public speaker, founder of non-profit organization and web designer. I have a strong desire to continue learning and learning and growing.

I am a person who is driven to achieve. I am not only a wife, mother, mentor, I am a spiritual person on a quest. I procrastinate on occasion, I love to have fun, I am serious, I am perceptive, and very intuitive, I have an opinion about certain things (everything), I love intensely, I feel the sorrow and pain of others as well as myself, I get depressed sometimes, I love the beauty of the mountains, I love Life!

Step 2: *Clear out the clutter!*

I did that yesterday and it feels GREAT!

Step 3: *What are you passionate about?*

LIFE! I am passionate about my projects – the OrphanConnect. com non-profit organization I founded, Magic of Intention products, coaching, counseling, teaching, learning, grandparenting, being a good wife to my husband.

Step 4: *Who or what drains your energy?*

Family issues, people who are less than sincere OR not honest with me, people and situations that are negative, long winters, loneliness, some people's inability to accept change as an opportunity for growth.

Step 5: *What risks are you willing to take?*

I have taken many risks in my life and as I get older I find that it's easier because I have nothing to loose but myself. I am willing to make cold calls to potential event planners who may be interested in my topic.

Step 6: *What gives you confidence?*

My husband, my friends, my clients. Knowing that I am on the right track

Step 7: *What have you always wanted to do or be?*

A writer and a motivational speaker.

Step 8: *What is the one action that would make your dream/ goal a reality? Writing NOW!*

———————

"Who we are never changes. Who we THINK we are does."

~ Mary S. Almanac,

Proclaimed Poet Writer

Meditation: Clarity is speaking (Write your experience)

Before starting your exercise, put on some soft music. Take a minute and close your eyes. Begin relaxing

Imagine that you are being bathed in a Sea of Clarity. You feel comfortable and loved in this sea.

You feel unafraid to be in the Sea of Clarity for you know the answers to your question will come swiftly and honestly.

Now open your eyes and write down what Clarity had to say.

Meditation: *(Sharing my experience)*

I am clear about who I am and what I want.

I loved being in the Sea of Clarity. I felt respected and believed in. All the little and big sea animals gave me wonderful advice and acknowledgement as to who I am and what I can and will do. I felt refreshed when I completed the meditation.

*The message is: I must be clear about who I am and what I want. I am clear that I want to make a difference in the lives of others. I must know who I am and what parts of me need to be healed. I am a mother, a wife, a teacher, a creativity coach, educated, inquisitive, fun, sad, happy, visual, and spiritual. I am 100% successful with all my projects and am a magnet for abundance. I know that I have to be prepared for all good things to happen, seek solutions to problems as they arise, grow personally and spiritually, and just keep on keeping on. The final message is: **Believe in yourself NOW!***

I hold my arms up in the air and
am grateful for who I am,
where I am going,
and all things around me NOW!

41

BELIEVABILITY

Chapter 5

We all have strong belief systems in the many areas of our life. And yet, the two areas that we most need to believe in is ourselves AND our dreams.

"Self-esteem is a way of being, thinking, feeling and acting that implies that you accept, trust and believe in yourself."

~ Peter Shepherd

Transformational Psychologist

In creating an intention, one must first of all, believe in ones Self. Hopefully you spent some time with the Steps found in Chapter 4 dealing with Clarity. In listing your achievements and positive attributes, you should have been able to realize what you have done in the past and what you can do now as well as the future.

It is very difficult to attain the desire you wish if down deep inside you…

a) do not believe in yourself and

b) do not really believe you can achieve your goal

Years ago I wrote a little ditty during a period when I was creating a support publication. I did not have a clue as to how I was going to develop it, but I was determined to create this publication. The name of the newspaper was *Divorce With Dignity* and my purpose in developing it was to help women see the "up" side of becoming single again.

Here are the words to the song – very simple.

I believe, I believe, I believe in me,
Won't you believe in ME?
I believe, I believe, I believe in you.
Won't you believe in YOU?
We believe, we believe, we believe in US.
Won't you believe in US?

~ Karin Janin

This simple little song carried me through a very tough time in my life.

Recently, I was able to teach this same song to a group of Special Needs Children and they quickly understood what it meant and loved it. The enthusiasm the children showed in singing this song reminded me of my own enthusiasm when I was first singing it. Do I truly believe in me? YES! Do I believe in you? YES! Do I believe in others? YES!

It is time to shout to the world "*I believe in me and in my dreams, my desires, my goals!*" Tell the world without fear of being made fun of... just shout as loud as you can. I have found that if you do not believe in yourself, it is very difficult to believe in your heart's desire. If you are not convinced that you deserve to achieve, then you will not convince others.

————————

"People become really quite remarkable when they start thinking that they can do things. When they believe in themselves they have the first secret of success."

~ Norman Vincent Peale

Minister, Author of bestseller,

'The Power of Positive Thinking'

————————

"There's no thrill in easy sailing when the skies are clear and blue, there's no joy in merely doing things which any one can do.

But there is some satisfaction that is mighty sweet to take, when you reach a destination that you thought you'd never make."

~ Spirella

Author

Life is full of surprises. It is exciting to step out of the box and do something that is satisfying. Something that brings back the passion that has always been there.

I have had many "can do" moments and it is those moments that pull me up when I am depressed that things are not happening as quickly as I would like them to do. Or when I am feeling the old stumbling blocks are "doing it to me again."

The satisfaction of completing, of just doing, of reaching a destination is oh, so sweet. I've traveled places that I have dreamed of but never thought I would really go. My life's experiences have been varied and I feel blessed because of the unusual opportunities that have been presented to me.

The following page gives you an opportunity to look at your old and new beliefs. Be honest with yourself. Keep in mind that as we change our beliefs change. So, from time to time, come back to this list and see if there is something new you would like to add or delete. You will be surprised at how much YOU have changed once you have read this book.

Enjoy the journey!

Exercise: *Old Beliefs & New Beliefs* *(Write your experiences)*

Old Belief	New Belief
(i.e., I am stupid)	*(i.e., I am brilliant!)*
I can't lose weight	*I am getting healthy now*

*Exercise: **Old Beliefs & New Beliefs** (continued)*

Old Belief	New Belief

VISUALIZATION

Chapter 6

Visualize – Imagine – See With Your Heart

In order to succeed, you must be able to visualize what it is you want to succeed in and to imagine that you ARE succeeding. Some people say they cannot visualize. If you cannot visualize, then feel what you cannot see. It works!

Imagination is another key to the Magic that opens a door to endless possibilities.

"Imagination is the beginning of creation; you imagine what you desire; you will what you imagine; and at last you create what you will."

~ George Bernard Shaw

Nobel Prize Laureate in Literature

Your desire is your destiny. Your will carries you through your imagination and you create what you desire.

By the time you are visualizing your goal, you have already done a lot of work. You are clear about what it is you want, you believe in yourself and what you want to achieve, Now it is time to get serious about visualizing! This is one of my favorite subjects because I know that if I keep the vision alive, it will happen. Maybe not always in the way I imagined, but the end goal does and will happen.

I remember years ago I visualized myself traveling and making money using my new found computer skills. I even made up name "Have Computer, Will Travel." I did not know exactly how it was going to happen, but I believed it would. I envisioned this when the desktop publishing business became popular and available for the everyday person. At that time I did not know what I know today about visualizing, being clear and believing... I just had a knowing.

It took about 10 years for my visualization to manifest, and it happened in a most surprising way. I was given an opportunity to travel all over Europe, designing presentations and training manuals for a group of environmental engineers. I was the only one with an Apple computer and design programs, so I was able to take my computer and printer to Europe for a year. How is that for visualizing a goal?

Through the years, I have learned to speed up the process even faster. I now have an attitude that "if it (my dream) can happen once, it can happen again." Of course, my dreams and goals have changed through the years. I am not the same person I was, so naturally my goals have changed.

The plus side of being a little older - my ability to visualize is better. I no longer have to wait ten years for my dreams to come true. Time is relevant. It passes quickly. Which means you can manifest your dreams faster if you understand the concepts I am presenting, work on the exercises, be clear about your intention, be persistent, and most of all believe in yourself. Step into the MAGIC.

Visualizing YOUR dreams, not the dreams of others, but yours is another key to the MAGIC OF SUCCESS.

"When you get right down to the root of the meaning of the word SUCCEED, you find it simply means to FOLLOW THROUGH."

~ F. W. Nichol

VP and General Manager, IBM

Now – it's time to do some visualizing.

Most exercises, meditations, and visualizations,

will include my experiences for you to read as an example.

Remember, we are not alike and your experience

will be different from mine.

Exercise: **How would you visualize your goal?** *(Write your experience)*

Today I visualize my goal as……..

Tomorrow I visualize my goal as…….

Next week I visualize my goal as …….

Next year I visualize my goal as…….

Meditation

Once you have answered the statements on the previous page, it is time to do some real visualizing.

Take a minute and close your eyes. Relax, breathing in and out slowly. Now imagine you are walking to a wonderful, safe place. And at that safe place, you have invited Merlin to your visualization experience.

Take a minute and ask a few questions. Listen silently to the answers. Now imagine Merlin taking the Magic of Intention Wand, swirling it around and around you. He stops suddenly and you can see through the mist of Magic to the future that is happening NOW.

Step into the Mist and FEEL every detail. What do you see? How do you see yourself? Feel the sense of empowerment. Be in the moment. You are in the VISION.

When you are ready, thank Merlin for this experience. Walk back through the Magical mists. Take with you all that you have learned about yourself and what you can do now!

When you are ready, open your eyes and immediately write down your experience.

Bring what you visualized into the NOW.

Meditation Experience: (Write your experience)

Exercise: (Sharing my experience)

Today I visualize my goal as............

An embryo in incubation. Writing down my ideas in my Magic of Intention Journal.

Tomorrow I visualize my goal as..........

Lost some sleep last night as I was excited about the project I have decided on. Am writing down all the ideas that I received during the night in my Magic of Intention Journal. It's time to do more research.

Next week I visualize my goal as…………..

Have started on my goal with enthusiasm. Have had a few interruptions due to family and clients but am staying focused. Felt a little discouraged, as I did not achieve as much as I could have. Have written three chapters in my book and sent those three chapters to my Editor.

Next year I visualize my goal as…………

My book is on the bestseller list! Being asked to be a keynote speaker. Omega Institute in Rhinebeck, NY asks me to teach a class on Magic of Intention, and are willing to pay my a large sum of money for my services. Also asked to go to Europe to "spread the word." Life is invigorating and fun! Meeting wonderful people all along the way.

FOCUS

Chapter 7

Staying focused means staying on track.

_____

"You can't depend on your judgment when your imagination is out of focus."

~ Mark Twain

American writer

By this time, you have an idea of what your goal is and maybe even a plan of action. But, we all have life's interruptions and staying focused is the hardest thing to do. I believe it is actually the biggest challenge we face.

---

*"**Focus** is channeled energy"*

~ **Perry A-**

Motivational Speaker, Author

My good friend Perry A~ speaks of focus as "channeled energy". It is exactly that, but sometimes there is a great deal of interference in those channels.

One of the reasons people have a difficult time staying focused is because they believe that they will have to give up certain things to achieve.

For me staying focused IS staying on track by setting boundaries. In setting boundaries, I can then channel my focused energy on the direction I want to go.

In our fast-paced world, it is almost impossible to work on our dreams every day. For example, recently I have had a large number of interruptions due to my husband's family and have had little time to work on this book. But, I have also been determined to spend a certain amount of time writing every day. I may say to myself that I will have three hours to apply myself to the book when, in reality, I have only an hour and a half to work on it.

There is no reason for me to feel badly about this because I keep my dream in front of me all the time. I may not be writing, but the words are running through my mind constantly. When a new thought comes to mind, I will quickly jot it down. Sometimes, when I am driving and cannot write down a new thought, I carry with me a small tape recorder and quickly record my thoughts. Every night I take a stack of books to bed with me to review them for new ideas on my subject matter.

So staying focused does not necessarily mean writing everyday, it means *holding the dream in front of you all the time.* It is sending channeled energy to the goal.

Sometimes we feel that if we do not place 100% of our focus on our dream, then it cannot happen. What we are actually doing is creating obstacles by worrying about whether or not we are 100% focused. No one is going to judge you but yourself. So let go of that thought and enjoy the process.

----

*"Only when your consciousness is totally **focused** on the moment you are in can you receive whatever gift, lesson, or delight that moment has to offer."*

~ Barbara De Angelis Ph.D.,
Relationship expert and author

As I mentioned before, I am completely focused on my dream through a variety of avenues – writing, researching, listening to my intuitive hits and talking to others.

So now I do not feel guilty if I am not "doing it right!" My style works for me.

"If you've lost focus, just sit down and be still. Take the idea and rock it to and fro. Keep some of it and throw some away, and it will renew itself. You need do no more."

~ Clarissa Pinkola Estes,

Author of 'Women Who Run With The Wolves'

The following page contains a focus meditation inviting the mythical Sea God – Nereus.

You may want to put on some soft music while reading this meditation.

If you have some meditative music with the sounds of the ocean, you may enjoy this more. Just enjoy and pretend.

Most exercises, meditations, and visualizations,

will include my experiences for you to read as an example.

Remember, we are not alike and your experience

will be different from mine.

Meditation: Focus

Breathe • Relax • Let Go • Enjoy

Imagine that you are on a wave, a calm soothing wave... perhaps in the ocean of the future. As you breathe in and out, so does the wave breathe in and out. Much like a cradle – holding you safely through the tides of life.

As you ride the waves, the mythical Sea God – Nereus, comes to you. Nereus was both very old and very wise and he has Magical answers to any questions you have.

Greet Nereus and spend a little time with him, for he has come up from the sea to help you focus.

Perhaps you would like to ask him how you can stay focused? Or what you should focus upon. This is your time with the Magical Nereus. Spend it wisely. Take about five or ten minutes or more if you wish. Feel the waves, know you're safe.

Now, the time is drawing to a close. Thank Nereus for helping you and, if you should want to call on him again, ask him if that would be ok.

Time to end this session and write down your thoughts on the following page.

Karin Janin

Meditation: **Focus** *(Write your experience)*

Meditation: *(Sharing my experience.)*

Ahhh... This really feels good to breathe, relax and feel the peace. I love the ocean so this particular exercise is quite inviting to me. I remember riding the waves and just letting them move my body. Up and down, with the sound of each wave rising and falling. Beautiful, beautiful sounds.

How strange, a mythical Sea God – Nereus is in front of me. He is so powerful and yet when I look into his eyes, I see wisdom and I am not afraid.

He welcomes me and I welcome him. We embrace and yet I am not sinking. It is as if the water is a comfortable waterbed, moving with my body in a fun way. I know that Nereus has come to me to help me and I accept his help for he has spent thousands of years in the ocean and knows what it means to focus.

I talk to him about focusing and he says "do you believe in what you are wanting to achieve?" I answer "yes." He says, "THAT is the most important thing."

He uses his spear and swirls the water around and says to me "focus on the center – the center of your inner power. That is all you need. Merge with the center that focuses and be with it."

He then vanishes into the sea.

ACT AS IF IT HAS ALREADY HAPPENED

Chapter 8

Prepare for the NOW!

Act as if it has already happened.

This is an extremely important concept. Acting "as if" your intention has already happened, reconfirms to your subconscious mind that YOU mean business!

---

*"When we believe something we **act as if it is true**; we have then made an investment of EFFORT... implies that you accept, trust and believe in yourself."*

~ Peter Shepherd

Transformational Psychologist

Let's say you intend to have the dream job you have always wanted. Perhaps you have already sent your resume out and then what?

Get ready. Go out and buy a new suit or dress, clean out your closets, *feel the emotion* of having that job. Ask yourself: "Do I accept, trust and believe in myself?"

Sometimes we do our focus work and act out "as if" we have the job, then someone else gets it. Perhaps this happens because the company you applied to is not the right one for you. If that happens, remember, something better is on its way. Continue being active by sending a resume to more than one company. This action keeps the energy flowing.

I know for me, whenever my client load starts to slow down, I get busy: I look around my office and notice what I need to thrown away; what I need to keep; I get organized; I research ways to market myself; and I use sage to release negative energy in the room.

I am upbeat and know that the universe will take care of me because I believe in what I am doing. I am constantly acting as if my client load is full and I am prepared for that. Even in pretending I have noticed that the phone starts ringing more. This is not a Pollyanna attitude. Researching your desired goal, staying focused, believing in yourself and your goal, and acting as if it has already happened brings the Magic to life!

Remember, our future is happening every second of the day. We have choices and opportunities. If you sit back and say, "I've done everything that you have said to do and still nothing is happening," then it is time for reassessment. In reassessing all your thoughts, words, and actions, you are in motion – always moving forward.

Be confident!

Being proactive is giving faith to your dream.

———————

"Part of being a good gardener is having faith in the seeds."

~ Anon.

———————

"Let him who would move the worlds, first move himself."

~ Socrates,

Greek Philosopher

Say YES to life!

In doing so, you will be saying YES to your dream!

Stop Sitting and Fretting

Start Moving and Being

Become the You That You Are

NOW!

"Sometimes you just have to take a leap of faith and jump."

~ Phyllis George,

Miss America - 1971, Author, Motivational Speaker

I see you taking that leap of faith

NOW!

"Thinking is easy, acting is difficult, and to put one's thoughts into action is the most difficult thing in the world"

~ Goethe,

German playwright

Achieving your goals does not have to be difficult. As long as you believe in yourself, believe in your goal and are willing to take action. Add a little Magical Passion and you are on the way to your success NOW!

Simply

ACT AS IF IT

(YOUR GOAL)

HAS ALREADY HAPPENED

Most exercises, meditations, and visualizations,

will include my experiences for you to read as an example.

Remember, we are not alike and your experience
will be different from mine.

Meditation: Acting as if it has already happened.

By this time I am sure you are used to the familiar words:
relax, breathe in and out slowly. So go ahead and make yourself
comfortable. Perhaps you would like to put on some soft music.
When I do this exercise, I like to listen to the *Chariots of Fire*. It
is a wonderful, empowering piece of music. I have used the music
Chariots of Fire in several of my workshops and the reaction is
always the same - empowering.

Now, just relax and imagine that you are acting as if your dream
or your goal has already happened. In your mind's eye, look around
your new environment, what do you see? What do you feel? Are
you excited, happy, grateful?

Imagine the activity happening around you. Feel your new-
found confidence rising to the occasion. How does that feel? Be in
the moment and know that these moments are real and are happening
NOW. Enjoy the Magic all around you.

When you are ready, come back to the present and write down
your thoughts, feelings, and actions on the blank page provided. A
sample of my experience has been included on the next page.

Meditation: *(Write your experience)*

Meditation: *(Sharing my experience)*

The music, Chariots Of Fire, is one of my favorite pieces because it builds empowerment.

You can feel the shift and the sense of success. I always feel empowered when I listen to it.

Looking around my environment through my minds eye, I see things that inspire, that remind me of success, that embrace love and peace.

There is a feeling of heightened excitement and a sense of knowing that everything will work. I need to be patient.

I love the power of the Magic around me – the Wand is swirling. Filled with powerful energy, flying in the air filled with tricks. But they are not ordinary tricks.

These are tricks that inspire, that build on each success, that share with others how to make their lives better, that reminds me we are all teachers and students.

Swirl, swirl, swirl.

Not in a dizzying way, but in a powerful manner. And the colors are both soothing and empowering.

I feel the music – it sings to me now. I am reaching the finish line – a Winner in all things!

ACCOUNTABILITY

Chapter 9

Accountability

This is the hardest chapter to deal with... as most of us would like to put off the task at hand. And we certainly would like to have someone else take responsibility for all or part of the work we need to do. It is very natural. But if we want to succeed and enjoy the Magic of our intention, we have to hold ourselves accountable. No one else can do what we need to do or can do!

Yes, we are great at creating, designing, affirming, intending, believing, visualizing, etc., but holding ourselves accountable is a little scary. That means, if something does not work or we do not follow through, we can only blame ourselves.

"**Accountability** *makes the process of change more tangible, more focused, more disciplined.*"

~ *Laura Whitworth*, *et al,*

Professional Life Coach, Author

When I work with clients and mention the word 'accountability,' there is often a funny look on their faces. *"You mean I have to do some homework?"*

The one thing I have learned in this lifetime is that I cannot walk in someone else's shoes… and they cannot walk in mine. For change to happen, for Magic to be complete, one must hold oneself accountable. In my own life, I have made a lot of mistakes and have been a great one for blaming others. The more I blamed, the more the negative situations occurred. I was just not getting it.

The "it" means I was not holding myself accountable. In other words, I was not learning my lessons. Believe me when I tell you that the Universe has kicked my butt more than one time. Luckily I started "wising up" and realized that nothing was going to change unless I did.

Change is necessary in ones life for personal growth. And holding yourself accountable is the best way for change to happen. I now welcome the opportunity to hold myself accountable.

You want to lose that unwanted weight? Well, that Magical diet will not work if you do not hold yourself accountable.

"I think there is something, more important than believing: Action! The world is full of dreamers, there aren't enough who will move ahead and begin to take concrete steps to actualize their vision."

~ W. Clement Stone,

Philanthropist, Author

Are you a dreamer or a doer?

Holding yourself accountable takes courage and I know you have it! You have always had it – the "it" is the Magic that has slowly been happening as you have been reading this book.

"If it is to be, it is up to me."

~ William H. Johnsen,

Foremost African American Artist

Honor the Magic and be armed with Accountability NOW!

"Like any art, the creation of self is both natural and seemingly impossible. It requires training as well as Magic."

~ Holly Near

Author, Activist, Teacher, Producer, Actor, Singer

Being accountable means being self-empowered. You too can feel the self-empowering moments that move you forward towards success. Remember, creation of who you are is both natural and possible. Holding yourself accountable, is the training that is required.

Yes, I know we as parents hold ourselves accountable for our children. Some of us even hold ourselves accountable for the nation or the world at large. We know that – in order to change the world, it must start at home and in our heart.

I remember, when I was working in Texas and experiencing emotional abuse at work, I felt that change had to happen. And that it had to start from the top down because it was the people at the top of the hierarchy of the business world who were our mentors, the people we looked up to. But in reality, the change had to happen within me. I had to understand what part I was playing in this scenario. It was tough, but I had to hold myself accountable for attracting such an intolerable situation. The good news is, I was finally able to leave that environment, never to experience that again.

So what is holding you back? Could it be the fear of the unknown?

"I discovered I always have choices and sometimes it's only a choice of attitude."

~ Judith M. Knowlton

Author

And how can that attitude be changed? Look in the mirror and ask yourself what it is you really want? What are you willing to do to reach and achieve the dreams that are a part of your destiny? What choices do you have?

"The time for action is now. It's never too late to do something."

~ Carl Sandburg

Author, Poet, Pulitzer Prize – 1940

It is never too late to take action and hold yourself accountable.

Are you ready and willing to see your dreams come true NOW?

The following page asks you to look at who YOU are by looking into an imaginary mirror. When I am working with clients I will sometimes ask them to imagine that they are looking into a mirror. I had one client who couldn't imagine looking in the mirror. Every time she would try, she couldn't see herself. This client had been emotionally and sexually abused and found it hard to see her authentic self who was loving, smart, innovative and caring. I had another client who "looked" in the mirror only to see her mother whom she despised. She too had been abused and had a difficult time seeing the "real person." Eventually she began to like herself and was able to imagine herself as the strong, independent person she saw in the imaginary mirror.

Most exercises, meditations, and visualizations,

will include my experiences for you to read as an example.

Remember, we are not alike and your experience

will be different from mine.

Exercise: Take a mirror and look deeply into it. (Write your experience)

What do you see?

A frightened person?

A victim?

A happy person?

How can you change that image to a positive image?

Are you ready to be accountable for <u>your</u> life and <u>your</u> intention?

Why?

Exercise: *(Sharing my experience)*

What do you see? *I see the wonderful ME that I can be and I am NOW!*

A frightened person? *At one time I was very frightened but not any more.*

A victim? *Well, yes, sometimes I want to blame others and get into the victim role, if things are not going right.*

A happy person? *I think I'm happy. Yes, I feel that life is on the right track for once!*

How can you change that image to a positive image? *Well, I've got to recognize what I've been doing and neutralize it so the negative things don't overpower me and take control of my life.*

Are you ready to be accountable for your life and your intention? *Absolutely yes! I am ready to "grow up" and hold my head high with pride. No more shyness.*

ROLE MODELS

Chapter 10

We all want and need role models. We have looked at our parents as role models, our teachers, our friends, the people we see in the media. We look for role models everywhere. Why? Is it because we want to be them or take on some of their traits, personality, achievements and incorporate that in our lives?

Role models are people we generally most admire. It is not your responsibility to become those people, but to learn what specific traits you admire and would like to develop for yourself. Always remember, you can only be YOU.

When you try to be something that you are not, then others will figure that out very quickly. The Magic is within you and for those people whom you admire, they too have discovered that their Magic is within them.

There are many, many people that I admire. Do I want to be them? No. I cannot do what they do, but I can do what I know best. For example, I admire my editor, Chelle Thompson founder of Inspiration Line. She is doing wonderful things through her online organization that inspire and bring joy to the lives of many all over the world. I too want to do that, but in my own way... as I can only be myself.

"A good example is the best sermon."

~ Benjamin Franklin
Inventor, Printer, Author, Politician

Another person I admire is Roger King from England. He had a rough beginning, but instead of feeling sorry for himself, he turned his sorrow, anger, and depression around to help others who have experienced emotional, physical and sexual abuse. He chose to become a counselor and help others in a field he was most familiar with. Now he is writing books, becoming a professional speaker, and carrying the message of hope out to the world.

I also admire my friend Perry A~ for her tenacity and her authentic self. Most of all, her humor – it's catching.

I admire my friend, Gay Smith, who despite the physical and emotional issues that she has to deal with on a daily basis, she is always there to give a helping hand. She is cheerful, perceptive and innovative.

My list of those I most admire is quite long. I cannot make a list without including my three children. They have done quite well despite their early years of trauma, disappointments, and losses. Without them I would not be where I am today and I thank them for that.

Something we must remember, there are two types of Role Models - Achievers and Non-Achievers. Yes, even non-achievers become our teachers. These people offer opportunities for our own personal growth. They remind us of what we stand for and what our hopes, dreams and ultimate goals are.

"From the errors of others, a wise man corrects his own."

~ ***Publilius Syrus,***

Writer of the 1ˢᵗ Century, B.C.

Time is on our side. Look around you and see who it is you admire. For me it is tough to say only one, as there are many. But for you, there may be only one. Honoring your role models is a celebration of life. Some role models are different and others are similar to who we are.

―――――――――

"A leader's role is to raise people's aspirations for what they can become and to release their energies so they will try to get there."

~ David R. Gergen,

U.S. White House advisor, journalist

Do not forget the most important person is YOU! Check where you have been, where you are now and where you are going. Give yourself a pat on the back. No more whining or complaining… for you are a *Star*. Better yet, you are a Magical Star!

―――――――――

"Share our similarities, celebrate our differences."

~ M. Scott Peck, M.D.

Author of the best-selling book
'The Road Less Traveled'

What would life be without Role Models? For me, it would be empty. I seem to need to admire others and I am hoping someday to make a difference in the lives of others so I can have the honored title of Role Model.

Before I end this chapter, I want to mention an experience I recently had at an airport. I was in Cincinnati catching the terminal bus which would take me to another terminal to catch my flight home.

I stepped into the bus, turned around and saw a young woman assisting two elderly people (a husband and wife) in wheel chairs. The young girl helped the woman out of her chair and then quickly turned to the husband to try and help him out of his chair. I looked at the elderly lady as she almost tripped getting on the bus with her cane. She looked at me, I asked if I could help. She graciously said no – with the warmest smile I have ever seen. Her eyes sparkled with love. They sat down where they could and the woman had nothing but positive things to say about her helper. I never heard either one of them complaining about their situation. They obviously saw the bright side of life.

When the bus reached the departure terminal, there were no wheel chairs immediately available. Once again, no complaining. I helped the woman walk a little before the wheel chairs showed up. They were both laughing, having a good time. Once in the wheel chair, she thanked me for helping and waved lovingly at me. They saw what I didn't see. They were grateful for the life they have and the opportunity to travel. And their eyes gleamed with pure joy! What a wonderful experience for me and I was blessed with new Role Models. Her last words to me were "Let The Good Times Roll!"

The following page is an exercise on Role Models, which will then move us into Part III, Obstacles.

Are you ready to

Let the Magic Roll NOW?

————————

Most exercises, meditations, and visualizations,

will include my experiences for you to read as an example.

Remember, we are not alike and your experience

will be different from mine.

Exercise: Role Models *(Write your experience)*

Take a few minutes and write down at least three people you most admire.

1.

2.

3.

and more if you want to….

Now look at your list. Determine what attributes would you most like to emulate?

What have you learned from them?

Exercise: (Sharing my experience)

Take a few minutes and write down at least 3 people you most admire.

My three children as I have mentioned before; Princess Diana; my ex-sister-in-law-Karen; Günther my biological brother in France.

Now look at your list and what attributes would you most like to emulate?

My children: Intelligence and Inner Strength

Princess Diana: Willingness to take a stand

Karen: Persistence

Günther: Inner Strength, Creativity

What have I learned from these people?

I've learned to be willing to change, to develop my inner strength, to forgive myself and others, to recognize that I have inner strength, to take a stand, be persistent in my dreams, work towards making a difference in the lives of others, and allow creativity to flow freely.

NOTES

PART III

OBSTACLES

Magic of Intention

SELF-DOUBT

Chapter 11

Talk about having a handicap... this is the biggest one! Self-Doubt takes you where no one else wants to go. It is destructive, manipulative, difficult to get rid of, and just plain ole nuisance! And we do this constantly to ourselves. I have experienced Self-Doubt many, many times and I am sure that I will experience it again. It can be very destructive and is extremely powerful! Self-Doubt shows up when you least expect it.

Just recently I was listening to an incredible speaker. She was full of energy, with a powerful voice, that carried a message. Someone I would like and admire. Then my ego went South! Yep – I allowed myself to think that I could <u>never</u> speak as well as <u>that</u> speaker I just heard. I immediately sent an email to my good friend Perry A~ who belongs to the same national speaking organization as this particular speaker, whining to her that I will never *be that* good! I was also intimidated by her membership in this very prestigious organization.

Of course, it was just like Perry A~ to pick me up by the britches and say: "*Hey Ms. Greatness... Don't let a little membership stop you from being a great speaker and delivering your message.*"

Once again, I was allowing Self-Doubt chatter into my emotional space.

In Life Coaching we call this critter that is, Self-Doubt, a Gremlin. And of course, with my vivid imagination, I see the Gremlin as a *Green Slimy Monster*. Do I want this *Green Slimy Monster to* stop me short of success?

"**Self-Doubt**... *stops progress.*"

~ Perry A-
Motivational Speaker, Author

Why do we allow Self-Doubt to creep into our lives just when things are going great? If you look at the whole picture, Self-Doubt is an obstacle and an illusion. The illusion is created by the Ego – the one that plays tricks with our minds. In Chapter 2, I discussed the Ego and the fact that we need a good healthy Ego. Yet, when our Ego stops us from achieving our goals and dreams, it becomes destructive. And Self-Doubt can destroy our chance for a brighter future in a flash.

How do we rid ourselves of Self-Doubt? I believe this is a life long process as we are challenged by Self-Doubt over and over.

The good news about the challenge of Self-Doubt is that it causes us to check-in with ourselves to determine just how dedicated we really are in creating our goals and dreams. The bad news is, we often let Self-Doubt derail our plans and miss the fruition of our efforts - those golden moments.

"Many of life's failures are people who did not realize how close they were to success when they gave up."

~ Thomas A. Edison

Inventor

Now let's get back to the concept that Self-Doubt is an illusion. How can that be? Well, look at all you have accomplished. Many of you have raised a family or have done things you never thought you would do. I received my under graduate degree when I was 51 years old and am presently working on my Ph.D. So we all know that we have achieved certain things. Give yourself some credit.

The key to letting go of Self-Doubt is to find a friend or someone who will be honest with you and will not let you sink into the mire of Self-Doubt which brings you down to self-pity. Having a good support group that will be there for you, "pull you up by the straps" and "set you straight," will make the difference. Remember the Magical person you are NOW.

You have choices: Do you want Self-Doubt to rule your life… to stop you on your journey to success? Or, are you ready to perform a little Magic and effectively whisk away Self-Doubt? It is up to you. What do you choose?

"Believe in yourself! Have faith in your abilities! Without a humble but reasonable confidence in your own powers you cannot be successful or happy."

~ Norman Vincent Peale
Minister, Author of bestseller,
'The Power of Positive Thinking'

What stops Self-Doubt? Confidence!
Believing in Yourself is the best cure.

"Man is what he believes."

~ Anton Chekhov,
Great Russian Storyteller

Most exercises, meditations, and visualizations,
will include my experiences for you to read as an example.
Remember, we are not alike and your experience

will be different from mine.

Exercise: Self-Doubt *(Write your experience)*

When was the last time you had Self-Doubt?

What was your reaction?

What did your inner chatter say to you?

Did you believe it?

If you did, then it's time for some quick Magic to happen. Are you ready? Imagine that the Gremlin is jumping all around your head. Now imagine that Magical Wand tapping the top of the Gremlin's and saying..."BEGONE WITH YOU NOW!" How do you feel now?

Exercise : Self-Doubt (Sharing my experience)

When was the last time you had self-doubt? *Just today while talking with someone about what steps were needed to get media attention for my non-profit organization, which is called The Orphan Connection.*

What was your reaction? *At first I felt overwhelmed! Not only am I trying to get others to notice a wonderful project with that organization, I'm also trying to complete this book in time for my publisher. Panic was the operative word for this situation.*

What did your inner chatter say to you? *The first thing I heard was, "Who do you think you are and who is going to care about the 'Bridges of Love Project' found on your orphanconnect.com web site? This story is about WWII pilots who protected the Belgium orphans at that time period. Now the pilots and the orphans are trying to reunite before it is to late as they are all much older." Then I heard, "You live in a rural community where people are concerned with everyday things, certainly not a reunion of old folks from WWII in Belgium."*

Did you believe it*? Yes, unfortunately.*

Now imagine that Magical Wand tapping the top of the Gremlin's head and saying… "BEGONE WITH YOU NOW!"!

Funny! I started laughing as I saw the little Gremlins running around and getting away as quickly as possible. They didn't like that Magic business at all! I'm actually laughing at the sight! Self-Doubt is out of my life NOW!

FEARS AND WORRIES

Chapter 12

I have read that fears and worries are basically the same concept. If you think about it they do work hand in hand.

When you worry, you are generally worried about something that may happen which is creating fear.

"We have nothing to fear but fear itself. "

~ Franklin D. Roosevelt

32nd U.S. President

Does fear come first or worry? *The chicken or the egg?*

We worry about our children getting hurt. But the worry is actually a fear that you will not be able to handle their being hurt.

----

*"Try a thing you haven't done three times before deciding its worth. Once, to get over the **fear** of doing it. Twice, to learn better how to do it. And a third time to figure out whether you like it or not. "*

~Virgil Thomson

American Composer

We are fearful about our future and therefore we are worried. I know I am. I turn on CNN every morning and my stomach has knots listening to what is going on in the world. It is scary. I do worry about the future of our nation and the world at large. Now, I'm even more fearful for my children and their children. I worry and am fearful about the possible outcomes. So, how does that serve me? It doesn't.

I realize that I cannot control others but I <u>can</u> be in control of my life. Watching the news every morning knowing that it is not positive does not help anyone psychologically, emotionally or spiritually.

To create a healthy environment, I am going to have to limit the amount of news I watch, and make my own news by seeing the beauty of my dreams and how, what I am doing, can make a difference in the lives of others. I must let go of the future and work on making personal changes one step at a time, one day at a time.

"The future belongs to those who believe in the beauty of their dreams."

~ Eleanor Roosevelt,

Activist and Former First Lady

Living fearlessly and doing what I love to do, is honoring who I am. And it is honoring who YOU are.

"You may be disappointed if you fail, but you are doomed if you don't try."

~ Beverly Sills,

U.S. opera star

I am not particularly fond of the word "try," but *fear of disappointment* holds us hostage and blocks the possibility of wonderful outcomes. We are doomed if we do not at least reach out to the opportunities that present themselves and create the person we want to be. Fear/Worry block us from our progress. Throughout our lifetime we will be faced with many blocks. Know that these blocks are merely stepping stones. How we deal with them is what makes a difference in the outcome of our future.

Ask yourself, "How does fear serve me? How does worry serve me?" Yes, I know we need to plan for the future and that is what you are doing now. The plan is for success and the realization of a brighter future. Your brighter future, your ability to reach your goal or goals, gives others the courage to do the same. See yourselves as Mentor Magicians through your own experience.

One of my favorite authors on fear is Susan Jeffers. She has a book called "Feel the Fear and Do It Anyway!" According to her, we often make fear the problem rather than the solution. If we looked for solutions, there would be no time to be fearful or worrisome. We would be spending our time, instead, figuring out how we can go from point A to Z.

A good example is that of mountain climbers. They are fearless. Why? Because they seek solutions for achieving their goals. Some of their solutions are to: stay fit, choose the proper equipment, study the terrain, prepare, prepare, prepare. Fear and worry is not on their agenda.

As human beings we, for some reason, tend to hold on to the greatest block we have and that is fear. Some have fear of success or failure. I know I have had that problem. Years ago I was given a test by a therapist who ultimately said that my biggest problem was my fear of success. I could not believe that a psychological test would show that. But there was the truth right in front of me. I had had a few failures and several successes but my focus was more on the few failures.

I can also remember, sometimes worrying – *"What if I become successful? What then? Will I be able to handle it? Will I have to travel so much, and be so tired that I can't answer questions properly? What if I'm not the greatest speaker or the speaker I was hired to be?"*

"What if" ruled!

Well, no more.

It has taken a long time and I hope it will not take you as long as it has taken me to let go of fear and worry.

"You gain strength, experience and confidence by every experience where you really stop to look fear in the face.

You must do the thing you cannot do. "

~ Eleanor Roosevelt,

Activist and Former First Lady

Look Fear in the face. Have a plan of action and seek solutions so the worries and fears stay far, far away.

There is a saying......

What you fear the most will come to pass.

Is that what you want?

I know I don't!

So it's time to use a little Magic and neutralize Fear/Worry. Are you ready?

---

*"Do not **worry** if you have built your castles in the air. They are where they should be. Now put the foundations under them."*

~ Henry David Thoreau,

Transcendentalist Author

Are you ready to do some foundation work? The following page has an exercise of fears and worries. Take your time and be honest with your answers. This is for you and only you unless you choose to share it with someone else.

Look at this as an opportunity for change, knowing that change brings new possibilities for a magical life.

―――――――

*"What's the use of **worrying**? It never was worth while, so pack up your troubles in your old kit-bag, and smile, smile, smile."*

~ George Asaf,

British Songwriter

Are you ready to pack your fears and worries away?

―――――――

Most exercises, meditations, and visualizations,
will include my experiences for you to read as an example.
Remember, we are not alike and your experience
will be different from mine.

Exercise: Fears/Worries (Write your experience)

If we choose to stay in the fear/worry mode, what is the payoff?

How does fear/worry serve you?

Now, close your eyes and imagine that fear and worry are popping up. Next, imagine that you're using the Magic Wand, swirling it around and neutralizing those thoughts until they are gone. How does that feel?

Exercise: Fears/Worries *(Sharing my experience)*

If we choose to stay in the fear/worry mode, what is the payoff? *It was the attention that I received. I'd hear my friends say. "I understand what you're going through. Maybe you should not take the risk."*

How does fear/worry serve you?

I feel that I have something in common with someone else who is also experiencing fear or worries. It's having a common bond.

Now, close your eyes and imagine that fear and worry are popping up. Next, imagine that you're using the Magic Wand, swirling it around and neutralizing those thoughts until they are gone. How does that feel?

Hmmm.

At first I was having a difficult time neutralizing Fear/Worry as I was so accustomed to having it in my life. But once I was able to neutralize it, I felt lighter, as if a something heavy had been lifted off my shoulders. My thinking is clearer. This is nice.

RESENTMENT, GUILT, VICTIM ROLE >> ANGER

Chapter 13

This is a another tough subject! I have spent several days fretting over this chapter . In writing this book I have had to look at my own issues and participate in the same exercises that you are working on while reading this book. I cannot honestly just talk the talk, I must also walk the talk.

Let's get into the subject matter.

Resentment	>>	Anger
Guilt	>>	Anger
Victim Role	>>	Anger

Resentment >> Anger

Who has not experienced resentment? I certainly have!

I have resented people who have had degrees (this was before I received mine), people who have had an easy life, unqualified people who have been in positions of power, my background.

But what resentment offers is: *anger, rage, and frustration.* These are not gifts of love, but of self-hate, of despair, and of sadness. I have been there… and I don't want to ever, ever be there again. There is no worse emotion than self-hate.

When we resent others, we are mirroring our own self-resentment.

"Anger is an emotional reaction when you feel out of control. It is used to intimidate, manipulate and even motivate. "

~ Perry A-

Motivational Speaker and Author

Resenting becomes a vicious circle.

Resentment >> Guilt >> Victimization >> Anger >> Resentment

When we feel resentful, we often feel guilty that we feel resentment.

We then feel victimized by our helplessness in the face of our guilty feelings. Then, we become angry and resent the *"forces* which made us feel guilty." Finally we are back to the original resentment.

We are **re-sending** to ourselves harmful, negative feelings that we think we are sending to someone else. Those negative feelings come in the guise of ANGER.

---

*"**Anger** will disappear just as soon as thoughts of resentment are forgotten."*

~ Buddha

Spiritual Teacher

---

*"**Resentment** is one burden that is incompatible with your success. Always be the first to forgive; and forgive yourself first always."*

*~ **Dan Zadra***

U.S. author

Guilt >> Anger

How many times have you felt guilty and then been very angry with yourself for feeling that way? Sometimes feeling guilty makes you feel childlike.

*"If I get **angry**, I will lose control, I am not safe. I will hurt someone! "*

~ Roger King,

Author, 'Soul Talk Stories.com'

Forgiveness is the Magical key. You will probably never forget what happened. But the inability to forgive keeps one blocked and stuck in anger and perhaps, feeling guilty about something you could not control.

"Persistent guilt feelings are destructive to self-esteem and area drain on our energies."

~ Healthy Self-Esteem

http://www.12steps2selfesteem.com/inside/html/lse-guilt.html

Finding a support group, a counselor or a life coach that will work with you on this matter is helpful. You are not alone in this, so please seek help. Do not let this rule your life. Take back your personal power NOW.

Victim Role >> Anger

I have mentioned the victim role several times in this book. This is an important topic and should be discussed because it is another obstacle to your success and it affects so many areas of your life. In feeling guilty, you may feel like a victim. You may feel like a victim when you are criticized or when you are full of resentment. All of these negative emotions affect the way YOU perceive who YOU are and they stir up the emotion of Anger.

We play the victim role well. Believe me when I say – I have played this role well. I played it so well, that I lost a lot of friends and more than that, I lost my self-respect.

I was angry at all the things that happened to me after my divorce from my first husband. I was living in Houston, Texas, at that time and had five car accidents – *all not my fault.* As soon as I was able to purchase "another car" I would have an accident.

So I would seek whoever would listen to my woeful stories. Needless to say, the new "listener" never stayed around very long. It took a while for me to figure out what was really happening. At a party one of my good friends said, after a few drinks, that it seemed like I was so unhappy that I wanted everyone else to be unhappy as well. That was a rude awakening.

There is an old saying – *misery loves company* – and as a person playing the victim role quite well, this may have been true for me. Thankfully, it is no longer true for me today.

*"Illness is in part what the world has done to a victim, but in a larger part it is what the **victim** has done with his world, and with himself. "*

~ Dr. Karl Menninger

American psychiatrist and author

Our outside world is generally filled with anger, but so is our inner world. Resentment, guilt, and allowing ourselves to be constantly criticized will cast us in a "victim role"... which always leads to inner ANGER.

*"Together they create and maintain the **victim** archetype."*

~ Colin C. Tipping,

Author of 'Radical Forgiveness'

>> Anger

Resentment, Guilt, Victim Roles are just a few of the areas that produce Anger. There are many ways to trigger Anger. Some of the ways are through media, politics, religious views, drugs, abuse, depression, and home life.

I recently counseled a thirteen-year old grief client who lost both parents due to Anger. The father was insanely jealous of the mother. He shot and killed her in front of his son. The police arrived and shot the father who still had the gun in his hand as they were fearful that he, the father, would kill his son. What a full circle of anger.

Anger begets Anger.

Anger is like poison that grows and grows. Yet it can be stopped if there is a strong desire to do so.

I think I could write an entire book about Anger. The sad part is that most people justify their anger; and yet ANGER is one of the greatest blocks we have to achieving our desires, our goals, our happiness, and our potential!

Ask yourself

What do you choose?

Anger or Peace and Calm

Personally – I choose LIFE!

Peace, Calm, Joy, Love

"Resentment *is the lack of self-confidence or recognitions of your own skills."*

~ Perry A-

Motivational Speaker and Author

The following pages will contain exercises to help you through the process of Resentment, Guilt, Victim Role, and several other obstacles that have not been discussed.

"Don't take anything Personally."

~ Don Miguel Ruiz,

Author, 'The Four Agreements"

———————

Most exercises, meditations, and visualizations,

will include my experiences for you to read as an example.

Exercise: **Resentment** *(Write your experience)*

What is it that I have always *Resented*?

What can I do about it?

How can I neutralize and transmute the emotion of *Resentment*?

Exercise: **Resentment** *(Sharing my experience)*

What is it that I have always *Resented*?

Honestly, I have always resented my adopted brother's success. Everything has come easy for him. I felt that my adopted mother loved him more than she loved me.

What can I do about it?

Let it go. So what? How does that serve me now? Well, it sure keeps my stuck and I am wanting to move forward with my life, not backwards! I choose to let go of resentment and start living my authentic life.

How can I neutralize and transmute the emotion of *Resentment*?

By seeing how insignificant it is to the whole picture of my life. I look at what I have accomplished. My journey is certainly different from his, but it is MY journey. I am proud of all that I have accomplished. So, I now place importance on the present and not the past – it no longer exists – it is neutralized in my minds eye and is transmuted to represent self-love.

Exercise: **Victim Role** *(Write your experience)*

What area in my life do I feel like a *Victim*?

What can I do about it?

How can I neutralize and transmute the emotion of Victimhood?

Exercise: **Victim Role** *(Sharing my experience)*

What area in my life do I feel like a *Victim*?

When there are issues being discussed within my husband's family and I am not included in it.

What can I do about it?

Get busy with my own business and don't worry about things that don't directly concern me.

How can I neutralize and transmute the emotion of Victimhood?

I transmute the victim role by taking charge of my life now.

The following pages contain exercises which include words that were not discussed but need your attention.

When you feel like it,
you may want to tackle the other negative emotions listed.

Exercise: **Grief >> Anger** *(Write your experience)*

What area in my life do I feel *Grief*?

What can I do about it?

How can I neutralize and transmute the emotion of *Grief*?

Exercise: **Frustration >> Anger** *(Write your experience)*

What area in my life do I feel *Frustration*?

What can I do about it?

How can I neutralize and transmute emotion of *Frustration*?

Exercise: **Betrayal >> Anger** *(Write your experience)*

What area in my life do I feel I have been *Betrayed*?

What can I do about it?

How can I neutralize and transmute the emotion of **Betrayal?**

Exercise: **Abandonment >> Anger** *(Write your experience)*

What area in my life do I feel *Abandoned*?

What can I do about it?

How can I neutralize and transmute the emotion of *Abandonment?*

UNABLE TO FORGIVE

Chapter 14

One of the greatest Magical keys to neutralizing and transmuting all those negative emotions I have mentioned in Chapter 13, is forgiveness. And yet, due to all of life's hurts, some of us are incapable of forgiving. We use that as a crutch to stay stuck.

I know from personal experience that forgiving someone who has hurt me is very, very difficult. But I have also learned that being unable to forgive creates even more problems for me. It is like a sore that never heals, and it's my sore…..no one else's.

Right now I am reading a wonderful book called *Radical Forgiveness* by Colin C. Tipping. I read parts of this book a few years ago, but for some reason I did not complete it then.

Now, I have picked it up again and am reading it cover to cover. I think it is time to do some serious work in this area. Remember, we are all teachers and students and as I have mentioned before, I am experiencing what you are experiencing in reading this book. We are working through our emotional "stuff" together.

Most of the self-help books I have read deal with, all or in part, forgiveness. Why? They recognize that this is a key Magical "potion," so to speak, that helps to heal the heart. This does not guarantee success, but it opens the doors. Some people say to me "but he/she did such awful things to me, how can I forgive and forget?" First of all, we are here on the planet to work through our lessons so that we can help others become whole and remember the spiritual beings we all are. This does not mean that you suddenly have to be buddies with the one that hurt you, but it allows you to let go of the emotion that binds you to what happened in the past and is keeping you stuck.

Years ago, I was raped by a man whom I did not know and who, I later found out, had raped other women prior to being sent to prison. After five years of good behavior (and prison overcrowding) this man was released. Within a month of being free, he raped seven women. I was one of those women. I was taken to a hospital for the necessary treatments. The police and medical personnel treated me with respect and concern, as I was traumatized. At the time, I had no medical insurance and could not afford professional help. So, needless to say, it took me years to forgive. But I did. I can honestly say

I feel nothing but pity for a man who has to rape.

———————

*"**Forgiveness** is the answer to the child's dream of a miracle by which what is broken is made whole again, what is soiled is made clean again."*

~ Dag Hammarskjold,

Swedish diplomat

It was a frightening experience. He had a knife in his hand the whole time and I felt my life in the balance. I clearly remember the experience, the exact time, and the emotions I was going through and yet, I have forgiven him.

———————

*"**Forgiving** is not forgetting. It is letting go of the hurt."*

~ Anon.

The child in me dreams and embraces the miracle of forgiveness. I will never, ever forget what happened. How can I? But I can forgive and let go of the hurt. Hanging on to the rage, anger, humiliation does not serve me. In fact, I give away my personal power to the hands of the man who hurt me if I dwell on what happened. That is not where I want to be. I want my personal power and I have chosen forgiveness as my Magical tool to move forward in my life.

---

*"**Forgiveness** is the giving, and so the receiving, of life."*

~ George MacDonald,

Novelist, Poet & Minister

Yes, it is difficult to forgive someone who has abused you emotionally and/or sexually. I understand that as I have experienced both.

---

*"The weak can never **forgive**. Forgiveness is the attribute of the strong."*

~ Ghandi,

Indian Spiritual/Political Leader and Humanitarian

Colin Tipping speaks of repression which is a way a person tries to forget a hurtful memory by "stuffing it" into the inner depths of their being. This action can wreak havoc later on in their lives later on.

I want to live my life to the fullest – and inviting anger, not being able to forgive, hanging onto resentment, is n*ot* living. To me, it is a slow, slow death.

And I am not ready to take that path.

I choose life NOW!

_____

"To succeed in life, you need two things: ignorance and confidence."

~ **Mark Twain**

US humorist, novelist and wit

Repression

After being raped, I immediately put my whole heart and soul into my little desktop publishing business. I thought that if I could just stay busy, then I would not think or feel what had happened to me.

_____

"When I repress my emotion my stomach keeps score."

~ **J. Enoch Powell**

Classicist and politician

Yet, I would find myself suddenly crying for no reason while working on a project. Down deep inside I knew that I needed help, but I could not afford to get it so I repressed the feelings that I associated with rape.

You know, rape is not just a physical event, it can be an emotional event as well. I have heard people feeling as if their minds had been "raped." I think one could relate mind raping to extreme emotional abuse. Rape is rape – it is taking away trust and empowerment, and the feeling of being violated exists for a long time.

Forgiveness is all empowering and heals.

---

*"The practice of **forgiveness** is our most important contribution to healing the world."*

~ Marianne Williamson,

Motivational Author

It takes courage to forgive and move on.

"Whether you be man or woman you will never do anything in this world without courage. It is the greatest quality of the mind next to honor."

~ James Allen

Author, 'As A Man Thinketh'

It also takes confidence to forgive and move on.

"As is our confidence, so is our capacity."

~ William Hazlitt

English Writer, Humanitarian Essayist

Ask yourself if you have the *Courage* and *Confidence* to forgive and let go.

The following pages contain an exercise on forgiveness. Take your time but be honest with yourself. In working on these exercises, you will be releasing the blocks to your success and will be able to reach your intended destiny.

Most exercises, meditations, and visualizations,

will include my experiences for you to read as an example.

Remember, we are not alike and your experience

will be different from mine.

Exercise: **Forgiveness** *(Write your experience)*

Make a list of all the people who have hurt you. Then focus on <u>one</u> person for this exercise. Once you have worked with one person, then you can work on the next person.

What happened to cause you so much hurt and anger?

Are you ready to go to the next step, which is forgiveness? If not, just write your thoughts down and when you are ready, you can move forward in this exercise.

Visualization: **Forgiveness**

Put some soft music on, turn down the lights, disconnect the phones and know that this is your time alone. Now, imagine you are among friends and family members whom you trust… and everyone is in a circle. If you would like, invite your Spirit Guide to join. Imagine that all are holding hands feeling the bond of love. In the middle, invite the one that has hurt you. Know that you are safe, surrounded by your support group.

When you are ready, go into the circle and speak to the person who has hurt you. Yell, scream, cuss, and say whatever you have always wanted to say. Remember, the circle of support that is there for you. Take your time. Feel the emotions. Ask the person why he/she did what they did.

Ask them if they had any idea on how much they hurt you and how that hurt has impacted present life. Hear the conversation between the two of you. If this becomes too difficult, simply become the observer and continue with the process. This is not easy, but you know the value of going through the wall of anger, rage, resentment, hurt and so forth.

Honor your emotional strength and courage in this process. Spend about ten to fifteen minutes in conversation with this person. Are you ready to forgive? Then go ahead. (If you are not, stop here and take a deep breath. Come back when you feel stronger and you have the confidence to forgive.)

When you have completed forgiving this person, thank him/her for the lessons you have learned– in particular, the lesson of self-forgiveness. In order to forgive others, we must be able to forgive ourselves. Now imagine that this person just disappears from your life, never to enter your conscious or subconscious space again.

Now that you have gone through this process, it is time to take one more step. And that is to walk over the Bridge of Love and embrace the emotion of unconditional love. Imagine that everyone in the circle rises and to the right is the Bridge of Love – the final forgiveness stage. Your friends and family who love and support you are there. But this time, you walk alone over to the bridge.

Take one step at a time as you get on the bridge. At the other end is your Spirit Guide who has been with you all this time. Slowly, with intent, walk the bridge and allow the feeling of healing emotions overwhelm you. Just close your eyes and let your Inner Guide take you to the other side. Your Spirit Guide is there for you. He/She embraces you with unconditional love. You have made a giant step and your Spirit Guide is so proud of you.

You are now given a Magical gift that will remind you of your own unconditional love. Take the gift, thank your Spirit Guide and say goodbye.

Meditation: *(Write your experience)*

Exercise: **Forgiveness** *(Sharing my experience)*

Make a list of all the people who have hurt you then focus on one person for this exercise.

Gerdi – biological Mom

What happened to cause you so much hurt and anger?

Orphanage-loneliness, lack of food, clothing, cold, loveless environment.

Circle Meditation

I have invited my three children, my husband, dearest friends, and my Spirit Guide. I breathe in slowly and invite Gerdi into the middle of the circle. Her English is "not so good," but I can understand her. I asked her why she put me in the orphanage. What happened in her life to do that? She began to cry – deeply wounded by my questions. I just stare at her. Then she tells me about her horrible situation after WWII and how her life, which had been good before, became a nightmare. She met what she thought was a wonderful American soldier who declared his love and she became pregnant. Instead of taking responsibility as he said he would, he quickly left

123

and went back to the United States as he had a family of his own. She never heard from him again She was penniless and with child. She had no choice. I looked at her softly, tears streaming down my face. I mentioned that I was in the orphanage until I was four years old. She said, she could not take care of me and that she had always regretted that. She begged me to forgive her, as she is an old, lonely woman now soon to make the transition. I continued to stare but my heart could no longer be hard towards her. I know I do not care for her, but I also know that her life has been a real Hell and that she could not take care of me. I am melting in the tears. It is time to forgive. I want to forgive because I do not want to harbor resentment and anger towards her any more. I looked at her. I then looked into her sorrowful eyes and said, in German - Ich vergebe Sie (I forgive you). She started crying and shaking and kept saying to me Vielen Dank, Vielen Dank, which means thank you. I then embrace Gerdi and forgive her and tell her thank you for giving me the opportunity to better understand what had happened.

It is done. She slowly disappears and I am fine. My heart is light and sings with joy. Joy, that I was able to talk with her. Joy that I was able to FINALLY let go of my anger and REALLY forgive her in my heart and to forgive myself for harboring resentment all these years. I have let her go, I have truly been able to let go of the past and I am ready to start living again. My circle of friends and family are overjoyed. I see them smiling and laughing and coming to me with congratulations. Hugging.

Now, my Spirit Guide reminds me that there is one more thing I must do and that is to walk over to the Bridge of Love. I stand straight, hold my head high and we all go to the bridge. I am reminded that I must make the trip alone, for no one can walk in my shoes. I look at my friends and family members then turn to step onto the bridge. It feels different – lighter than I thought it would, or perhaps I am lighter. I now realize that being able to forgive has lightened my body, heart and soul. I am singing as I walk across. I see my Spirit Guide on the other side. We embrace once again. But there is something different. My Spirit Guide has grown in stature and the light surrounding her is wonderfully, lovingly bright. She hugs me and I feel even more healing coming through her arms. I feel safe. She reminds me that I have taken a huge step and she is very proud of me. Now, I must share this with others. Now, I can give myself the gift of unconditional love, for it comes from within. That is the gift she gives me. I feel like I am being bathed in love and I close my eyes. When I open them again, I am on the other side of the bridge and the bridge disappears. In awe of what wonderful Magic has just occurred. This is wonderful and I am

FREE TO BE ME NOW!

Frei, mich zu sein

Libre de M'Etre Maintenant!

"Forgiveness means letting go of the past."

~ Gerald Jampolsky,

Motivational Author

INABILITY TO LET GO

Chapter 15

Throughout this book you have seen the words, "letting go."

Letting go of Anger • Letting go of Frustration

Letting go of Anxiety • Letting go of the Need to Control

This chapter is about our inability to let go of emotions that become obstacles in our progress and no longer serve us.

So why do we have such a tough time letting go of things that are obviously unhealthy for us? The things that are holding us back, and becoming a huge obstacle in living a successful and authentic life?

I have found that one of the answers to this puzzles is that we are so accustomed to being unhappy, to being in an unhealthy relationship, to being in a job from hell, that we are afraid to take a risk and step out of what we are accustomed to. Part of us may be afraid that "this may happen again."

It is so strange that we are willing to stay in situations that drain our energy. And yet we do it all the time. I understand the fears of stepping out of unhappiness. Subconsciously our self-esteem is low, our fears are great and we imagine the worse that can happen. I remember when I wanted to divorce my first husband. I told my mother about my unhappiness and the fact that he was emotionally abusive. She said to me "but Karin, he comes home to you everyday and he makes a good living." I was disappointed that she was not supportive of my decision, yet I knew that I had to do something. For ten years I was unable to let go of this unhealthy relationship. And when I did, it was scary. I knew it was a risk and I took it anyway.

If we don't take risks and step out of our comfort zone, letting go of what is NOT good for us, then how can we help others in their unhappiness?

I had to let go of an unhappy marriage years ago. Although I had three small children I could not stand the emotional abuse any longer. Did I feel empowered being the one who initiated the divorce? Yes and No. I was a frightened young divorcee in a "brave new world" and I did not have a clue as to how the children and I would survive.

Now there is a difference between being unable to let go of certain unhealthy emotions or situations, and just letting to of things without putting enough thought into the end results.

There have been time when I was able to let go of certain situations when, in fact, I should have thought it out. Yes, I can freely admit that from time to time I have not been very responsible in my "letting go." In other words, I feel that I didn't think it through. In some situations, I had others to consider and I regret that.

But this chapter is not about regrets, it is about not being able to let go of unhappy, unhealthy emotions or situations. The self-destructive ones.

For example, I am not encouraging you to quite your job because you are unhappy. I am encouraging you to seek solutions to your present situation.

What I am trying to say, is that sometimes we are unable to let go for all the wrong reasons. Generally we are afraid to take a leap of faith and trust our intuition. Discernment is a key that will help you decide what you need to let go of. When you finally do, door open. There is a saying "When one door closes, the other opens." I see this a little differently:

"Walk through the door that <u>has always</u> been open, for the closed door is already shut tight."

~ Karin Janin

The door of opportunity has always been there for you. It has been opened for a long time just waiting for you to go in. Instead, most of us have one foot in the door that is about to close and one foot in the door that is already opened.

Letting go of emotions that no longer serve you and are blocking your progress is what this chapter is referring to. What are we holding onto? Pride? Control?

―――――――

*"To be able to **let go**, we need to be able to recognize when we are holding on to something and on what level."*

~ SacredSmile.com

Once I have let go of whatever it is, I hold myself accountable for my actions, and go on with my life. We have been given an opportunity to take charge of our lives and the "ritual" of letting go moves us in the direction of being proactive with change.

Part of forgiveness (which was discussed in the previous chapter) is letting go of the emotional attachment that has held you in a negative state and that no longer serves you.

―――――――

"There are seeds of self-destruction in all of us that will bear only unhappiness if allowed to grow."

~ Dorothea Brande

American Author & Editor

Are you unable to let go of the things you are unhappy about? Remember, the seeds of unhappiness grow quickly. So it is time to tend to your inner garden and let go of the weeds of self-destruction.

Most exercises, meditations, and visualizations,

will include my experiences for you to read as an example.

Remember, we are not alike and your experience

will be different from mine.

Exercise: **Letting Go** *(Write your experience)*

Think about a few things you would like to let go of and you are having a difficult time doing? Could it be an attitude? A relationship? A job? A friend? An expectation?

Get to the core of why you want to let go of _____.

Can you imagine Letting Go of _____ as an opportunity to seek alternatives?

What are you resisting?

Exercise: **Letting Go** *(Sharing my experience)*

Think about a few things you would like to let go of and you are having a difficult time doing so?

For me it is an attitude. I'm afraid that I may not make my publishing deadline date for this book.

Get to the core of why you want to let go of _____.

The core is fear of not meeting my deadline. Well, maybe it's deeper. Fear that no one will read this book and so having a fear about meeting the deadline date is masking my fear of rejection.

Can you imagine Letting Go of <u>*not completing this on time*</u> **as an opportunity to seek alternatives?**

Yes, I know better. My focus should be on doing the best job I can do. And to believe that I actually have all the time I need.

What are you resisting?

Self-control. In reality, sometimes I waste more time on things rather than focusing on this project.

I AM in control NOW!

---

*"Truly loving another means **letting go** of all expectations. It means full acceptance, even celebration of another's personhood."*

~ **Karen Casey,**

Meditations Author

Meditation: Letting Go

Find a place where you are most comfortable. Once you are comfortable, begin relaxing all parts of your body, your muscles, your calves, all the way up to the top of your head. Now imagine the thing that you are having a difficult time letting go of. Feel the emotion connected to that.

All emotions are connected to some part of your body. Find that part of your body. Get in touch with that part of your body. Name that part of the body that holds the thought of not wanting to let go of_____.

Are you ready to let go of whatever you are holding onto? Great.

Now, it is time to identify whatever it is you are holding onto that is not good for you. Grab it with the loving arms of "Letting Go." Imagine the thought being pulled out of a particular part of your body... gently, but with determination. Letting Go is working with you, so you can be open to new opportunities. Continue imagining that Letting Go is pulling out both resistance and whatever it is you are now truly letting go of. Keep pulling, keep pulling, almost there. And once it is out, replace it with the perfect alternative.

Relax....come back to the present and see your new alternative working for you now!

In this space, write down your experience.

RESISTANCE TO CHANGE

Chapter 16

" *I'll change...really I'll change but.........*"

How many times have you said that to yourself <u>and</u> *nothing* changes?

I am married to a wonderful man, yet he has issues with change. At least now he will freely admit it – that's an improvement.

I have jokingly told him many times that this is why I am in his life.

Before we were married I told him that if I was going to live in the house he and his ex-wife lived in (ladies, this not a good idea – start fresh), I was going to make a lot of changes with the décor inside and out. The house has been full of negative energy and my tastes are different. He said "that's fine."

But when I started throwing away things – rearranging furniture, making plans for renovations, his mood changed quickly. He became withdrawn. I reminded him that we had an agreement <u>before</u> we were married that this was going to happen and that we agreed I would create a house that had OUR energy in it.

----

*"**Change** is inevitable. **Change** is constant."*

~ Benjamin Disraeli,

British Prime Minister

He conceded we had made that agreement <u>before</u> getting married and now he's very happy with the changes. The house is "lighter." Some of the depression has been lifted. Not all, of course, after all, Rome was not built in a day! There was no point in going overboard. Taking baby steps and giving him time to readjust was what worked best for him… and in turn, for me.

Another example of resistance to change comes from a good friend of mine in Texas. Her name is Ellie. Ellie's job was in procedural writing and she liked parts of her job, although it was very time consuming. Her work environment was awful. The amount of emotional abuse she put up with for four years had taken a toll on her physically and emotionally. Why? She was resistant to change.

You may ask "Why would someone continue to work in that kind of environment?" I asked her that many, many times. She would give excuses like: job security, paid time off to take care of her ailing mother, health insurance, etc. There were times when she would get completely frustrated and only then would she create a new resume or look in the newspaper for a new job. But, it didn't take long for Ellie to get back into her old pattern, which was being comfortable in a miserable situation. Ellie resisted change for four long years.

---

*"**Change** is inevitable. **Change** for the better is a full-time job."*

~ Adlai E. Stevenson,

U.S. Vice President

Well, when you keep resisting change, the Universe will take care of it and force YOU to change. That is exactly what happened to my friend. She was fired from her job.

Make change YOUR friend!

"The time to repair a good roof, is when the sun is shining."

~ John F. Kennedy,

35ᵗʰ U.S. President

For Ellie, the sun was no longer shining and her well-being desperately needed repairing. She was finally forced to look for a job elsewhere. My good friend developed an excellent resume, went on a job interview and was immediately offered a job on the spot with *more* money than she was making before.

Why did it take her so long? Why does it take any of us so long to change and to realize that change is not going to happen *out there,* but *inside ourselves* where everything begins? She and so many of us are not willing to listen to what is going on INSIDE.

"If you are not listening, you are NOT learning."

~ Lyndon B. Johnson,
36ᵗʰ U.S. President

We make excuses: we need the job, we need the security, we need this or that relationship, we need to be the caretaker for everyone, and so forth. All the while we are miserable. We are NOT listening to our inner wisdom. What does it take to awaken?

I know many people who will not listen to their inner wisdom and suddenly become physically ill, or lose their job, or their marriage, or have to leave their 'comfort zone'. If there is something going on with your body, listen to the inner wisdom – see a doctor, go on a diet, change habits that are not working for you. If you are having problems in your marriage – seek professional help, learn to communicate, be willing to make changes.

––––––––––––

*"Be the **change** that you want to see in the world."*

~ Mohandas Gandhi

Indian Spiritual/Political Leader and Humanitarian

Resisting change creates what we talked about before: *resentment, anger, fear, frustration, and so forth.* The more you resist, the less energy you have. You may feel emotionally or physically drained. You may be depressed all the time. You may be taking harmful substances to mask your personal pain.

––––––––––––

*"**Change** in all things is sweet."*

~ Aristotle,

Greek Philosopher

Taste the sweetness of change. Personally, I have gone through so many changes that I now invite CHANGE into my life. Why? I have learned that change is an opportunity for growth.... personal growth from the inside out!

---

*"The key to **growth** is the introduction of higher dimensions of consciousness into our awareness."*

~ Lao Tzu,

Chinese Taoist Philosopher

Change offers us an opportunity not only for personal growth but spiritual growth, as well as getting in touch with the Infinite Source and having an awareness of life all around you.

How long has it been since you noticed a sunset or a sunrise? Change your schedule and start looking at the beauty and wonderment all around you.

How long has it been since you've been childlike, playful and laughed while rolling down a hill?

---

*"You must take personal responsibility. You cannot **change** the circumstances, the seasons, or the wind, but you can change yourself. That is something you have charge of."*

~ Jim Rohn,

Motivational Author & Speaker

Are you ready to stop resisting change and start living?

When you have completed the following exercise on "change," may I suggest a new mantra that will help you change? Say this several times a day until you feel you have embraced change. Or say it when you are questioning your present situation.

Change is my Friend • Change is my Friend
Change is my Friend • Change is my Friend
Change is my Friend • Change is my Friend

—————————

Most exercises, meditations, and visualizations,
will include my experiences for you to read as an example.
Remember, we are not alike and your experience
will be different from mine.

Exercise: **Resistance to Change** *(Write your experience)*
What one thing would you like to make an immediate change in?

What are the obstacles that are keeping you from making a change?

Check in with your energy level? How would you grade it?

How can you Change the obstacles?

What is the first step you would take to make just a little change? Baby steps are ok.

When you are ready dissolve <u>Resistance</u> from your vocabulary and embrace CHANGE. Say to yourself. I intend to CHANGE NOW. (*In Part IV you will learn how to be more specific with your intention statements.*)

Exercise: **Resistance to Change** *(Sharing my experience)*

What one thing would you like to make an immediate change in? *Stop avoiding the things I need to take care of immediately.*

What are the obstacles that are keeping you from making a change? *Me and Me. I need to change my attitude. I feel like a child kicking and saying, "Tomorrow, tomorrow I will do it."*

Check in with your energy level? How would you grade it?

I would grade my energy level regarding what I must do at 30%.

How can you Change the obstacles?

By changing MY ATTITUDE about the things I need to take care of. These things will not take that much time out of my life, for goodness sakes! I am spending too much time in avoidance.

What is the first step you would take to make just a little change? Baby steps are ok. *Make a list and checking it twice (Santa's premise). I intend to be proactive in what needs to be done now.*

I no longer waste time wishing and hoping – I am doing NOW!

LOOKING BACK

Chapter 17

If only....

If only I had done this or that.

If only I had paid attention....

If I had done this, then this would not have happened.

If only.....

Have you made any of these statements? I know I have more than one time in my life!

There is a Biblical story about Lot and his family fleeing the cities of Sodom and Gomorrah to escape God's wrath. They were warned to not look back or they would be turned to a pillar of salt.

Lot's wife did not believe the messenger so she looked back. She was immediately turned to a pillar of salt.

Now, this is not going to happen to you, but looking back can only keep you stuck like the pillar of salt unless you choose to look forward.

---

*"Change is the law of life. And those who **look only to the past** or present are certain to miss the future."*

~ John F. Kennedy,

35th U.S. President

The message this book is trying to impart to you, the reader, is that we need to let go of the past, stop looking backwards and start looking forwards to the future. Who we are now is what counts and that requires liking ourselves.

---

*"**Self-acceptance** is a practice, a willingness to slowly expand our ability to see ourselves as we are and simply be with what we see."*

~ Oriah Mountain Dreamer,

Author, Speaker

I now tend to have a "who cares" attitude about the past. But it took me a long, long time to develop that. Our past is a story, and like so many stories the "outcome" can be different from the beginning. The "outcome" is our present and our future. It is what WE clearly decide it will be.

Yes I know, we are all affected by the outside world. We would not be human if we were not. Our past is OUR PAST and the most important lesson to learn is to understand, forgive, let go and move on.

I know people who say things like "everything bad happens in three's." Hence, they continue to be guided by a few past experiences and so their self-fulfilling prophecy will and does happen over and over. These people are looking to their past to validate their present experiences. It is as if they are waiting for bad things to happen. Are you one of these people? Do you know people like that? Obviously, this is not a healthy approach to life and happiness.

"Others can stop you temporarily. Only you can stop yourself permanently."

~ Patti Kaprelian,
Professional Success Coach

You are in control of your life. You cannot change or control others but you *can* change and control yourself. The past is the past is the past.

There was once a wonderful, fun movie called "Back to the Future." We cannot really go back to the future. We cannot undo what painful events that we have experienced. We cannot rewrite the script. That was just a movie about an impossible fantasy. We can, however, write a future that is happening now. Every new second is a new future that just happened.

"If you spend your life looking in the rearview mirror of life, you will surely have a collision with what lies ahead."

~ Jordan Jankus,

Special Needs Director

Each moment is made up of our reality. What is real is this very moment in your life. What is not real is what has already happened. It is gone, over with. It is important to not miss a beat of life – each moment counts.

---

*"Guard well your spare **moments**. They are like uncut diamonds. Discard them and their value will never be known. Improve them and they will become the brightest gems in a useful life."*

~ Ralph Waldo Emerson,

Author, Poet, Philosopher

Talk to someone that is terminally ill. They live in the moment because they know that is all they have.

147

---

*"It is in your **moments** of decision that your destiny is shaped."*

*~ **Anthony Robbins,***

Motivational Speaker

What is your decision?

Live for the "what ifs"?

Or

Embrace the present moments that lead to your destiny?

Make a decision – backwards or forwards?

---

*"In a **moment** of decision the best thing you can do is the right thing. The worst thing you can do is nothing."*

*~ **Theodore Roosevelt,***

26th U.S. President

The following pages contain an exercise that will help you understand your past and move you into the present. It is living in the NOW that counts, not all the yesterdays.

Most exercises, meditations, and visualizations,

will include my experiences for you to read as an example.

Remember, we are not alike and your experience

will be different from mine.

***Exercise:* Looking Back** *(Write your experience)*

When you are looking into your past what do you see?

How has "looking back" kept you from "looking forward?"

How can you live in the moment? Try it and write your experiences down.

How did it feel to be in the moment?

From this day forward make an agreement with yourself to live in the present and seek to move towards a successful future. Handwrite or type your agreement, print it and put it some place where you can be reminded often.

Exercise: **Looking Back** *(Sharing my experience)*

When you are looking into your past what do you see?
Failure.

How has "looking back" kept you from "looking forward?"
It certainly has kept me in a state of fear that no one will approve of what I am doing. So I have carried my fears and self-doubt into the present and it has kept me from reaching my potential.

How can you live in the moment? Try it and write your experience down.
Be aware of each moment. Actually, this caused much of the sadness to be lifted.

How did it feel to be in the moment? *It feels good. The sadness seems to be lifting out of me, although self-doubt crept in for a minute. I told it to leave as it is impeding my progress in the present.*

From this day forward make an agreement that you will live in the present and seek to move towards a successful future.
I DID!

I DID!

I DID!

I DID!

KARMA
WHAT GOES AROUND – COMES AROUND

Chapter 18

What goes around, comes around.

You do good deeds, someone else will do a good deed for you. You steal from someone, someone else will steal from you.

There is an old song by Harry Chapin called the *Cat's In The Cradle*. This is a very powerful song. If you have not heard it, please do so. It is a song about a young father who is so busy being a good provider, moving up in a company, that he has no time for his son. His son grows up, the father retires and finally has time, but the son now has his own family to take care of and no time for the father.

Words are powerful and words can hurt. This young son was hurt and now he is subconsciously hurting his father because of the role model he saw as child….. *"I'm too busy…not now…soon…"*

Let me say this again:
Words are powerful and words can hurt!

Debbie Ford, author of *The Dark Side of the Light Chasers,* has written that we all have shadow personalities. Those personalities that we don't like, that are somewhat negative and untrustworthy.

Robert Assogioli, father of Psychosynthesis, talks about this as well. We cannot ignore these sides of our personalities, but we can acknowledge that they exist and realize their impact on our judgments.

"If you don't own up to a dark part of yourself that mistrusts other human beings, it will own you and in various ways run – and then ruin – your life"

~ Robin Sharma, best selling author
The Saint, The Surfer, and the CEO

When we say something hurtful, it will come back to haunt us unless we acknowledge our action.

I am almost embarrassed when people say kind things to me about who I am because I know that I have a very dark side. I am sometimes quite tactless and I do not mean to be. Some people think I am very clever in the things I say because I am quick, yet sometimes my remarks can be very hurtful. If I have been tactless to someone, someone else has done the same thing to me.

Let's talk about the concept of "What Goes Around, Comes Around" better known as Karma. Many people equate Karma with past-lives. Personally, I am not 100% convinced about past lives and I am not going to get into a long discussion about it. Many people become so fascinated with the character they think they were and lose sight of the true value of a past life experience. The purpose of going through one is to release or better understand ones fears, emotions, or personal traits. I do believe that there are emotions attached to the "past life story." And it is those emotions that need to be worked through.

In Karma, one believes that they may have done something bad (or good) and they are "paying" for it or being rewarded for it now. I once had a terrible relationship and when it was over I thought to myself, Karma will happen to this person. He was emotionally abusive to me so therefore, I assumed someone else would be emotionally abusive to him. How silly for me to wish that on him and to want to wait for it to happen. In doing that, I took precious time away from living the kind of life I could have been living. The unproductive time was spent on my anger and frustration.

Let's talk about self-discovery. Self-discovery is discovering WHO YOU REALLY ARE. If it takes a past-life regression to do that, then go for it! Just remember what you are trying to discover. Not the character or persona, but the emotions behind the character that may be influencing you in the present. I am certified in this field and have seen wonderful emotional healings happen, but only because the individual was ready.

As I said before, getting caught up in the past life character delays the self-discovery in the emotion. Once a client understands what brought them to where they are now, they can then move forward. They can let go of the emotion that binds them to the obstacles in their life. "Past Life" emotions often mirror the "past" in the life currently being lived. Past-life regression is a wonderful tool for the right reasons. If you want to go through this experience, please make sure that the person you are seeing is certified!

Remember that Karma works all the time. If you steal, someone will steal from you. If you are mean, someone will be mean to you. Be aware of negative Karma and stay clear of it.

We are human and as humans we do things without thinking about them. Simply be aware of what you may be doing. You'll be surprised how well your life flows.

———————

"Remember who you are, she said. You're a master."

~ Aniesa Thames,

HarmoniousEarth.org

Most exercises, meditations, and visualizations,

will include my experiences for you to read as an example.

Remember, we are not alike and your experience

will be different from mine.

Exercise: Karma *(Write your experience here)*

What kind of Karma have you experienced? Have you said something that came back to "haunt" you?

How have you dealt with it?

What can stop you on your tracks and prevent negative Karma from happening again?

You're quickly becoming a

***Master Magician* in your life.**

Exercise: Karma (Sharing my experience)

What kind of Karma have you experienced? Have you said something that came back to "haunt" you?

In my younger days when I was going to college, I was asked out on a date. Actually, I made two dates for one night. I had to choose and I chose the one who would be "fun." I called the other up and said I was sick. I went out with date number one and number two date caught me lying and that was the end of the relationship!

How have you dealt with it?

I was embarrassed because I actually liked the fellow I lied to. I tried to make up excuses but he didn't buy into them. I never did that again.

What can stop you on your tracks to prevent negative Karma from happening again?

Remember, if I hurt someone, someone else will hurt me the same way. Instant awareness before something happens.

You're quickly becoming THE

***Master Magician* of your life.**

YES I AM!

OPPOSITES ATTRACT
MEDITATION

Negative to Positive

Magical Intentions are happening
NOW without you even knowing.
Your life is changing in the twinkling of an eye and the swirling
of the wand.

With each chapter I discuss what the topic is and then I include an exercise, a meditation or a visualization for you to work on.

I wanted to do something different as a way to end Part III on Obstacles, in order to bring it all together. So I have created a meditation called *Opposites Attract*. It is somewhat long but quite powerful.

The purpose of this meditation is to neutralize and/or transmute the obstacles in your life so you may move forward quickly.

Exercise: Opposites Attract *(Write your experience)*

Step 1:

Take a deep breath and relax. Now imagine what you need to do to make your life better. What goals would you like to see happen in your life (i.e., a new job, attract a relationship I deserve, the house of my dreams, etc.)? Now use the space below to write your answers.

---

*"I was not looking for my **dreams** to interpret my life, but rather for my life to interpret my **dreams.**"*

~ **Susan Sontag,** *Renowned American Author*

Step 2:

Now look at the obstacles (self-doubt, fears/worries, resentment, anger, frustration, criticism and self-criticism, betrayal, grief, depression, rage, victim role, or any other obstacle that is on your personal list). Ask yourself why your not living the life you want? What is keeping you stuck?

Step 3:

Now look at the obstacles (self-doubt, fears/worries, resentment, anger, frustration, criticism and self-criticism, betrayal, grief, depression, rage, victim role, or any other obstacle that is on your personal list). Ask yourself why your not living the life you want? What is keeping you stuck?

Step 4:

Time to face the music. Look at your greatest obstacle… the one that is keeping you from your destiny, which is success. The obstacle I have chosen to work with is _____

_____.

Step 5:

Each word has an opposite meaning. For example:

> **Frustration – Satisfaction (opposite)**
>
> **Betrayal – Loyalty (opposite)**

Abandonment – Embracing (opposite)

Victim Role – Empowerment (opposite)

Grief – Joy (opposite)

Anger – Love (opposite)

Resentment – Admiration (opposite)

The Dictionary or Thesaurus may not agree with this list, but it works for me. Whatever positive opposite word works for you is what you should use. Remember, we are going from negative to positive. You are doing great. Now it is your turn:

Negative - to - *Positive*

Step 6: Visualization

Time to call in reinforcements. (You may want to tape this part of the meditation) Close your eyes and imagine the obstacles you are working on. Imagine the Magician in you waving its wand and saying wonderful, magical, powerful words. It is neutralizing the control this obstacle has over you. Feel with your senses, imagine with your inner vision, sense the power of the Inner Magician. The negative energy of those words are neutralized and transmuted to the wonderful powerful opposite NOW. Feel the energy inside of you becoming stronger and stronger because you are becoming stronger and stronger. Just be in the experience. Know that this obstacle no longer has influence or control over your life. You are Free of it. Go to your heart and sense its relief, and release of the burden the obstacle put on it. Feel your body getting lighter and lighter. Imagine that it is swirling in an upward motion. Feeling so good, so powerful, so in control. See the Inner Magician placing the sacred Magician's hat on your head, for you have passed the test of time and are now an honored Magician of Intention apprentice. Feel the good feelings, the strength behind the words. Know that you have the ability to change what you want to change. Slowly come down and start to ground yourself to Mother Earth, who is another Magician.

When you are ready, open your eyes.

Step 7:

When you know that the negative obstacles you just worked on no longer has any power over you. And, when you have time, or as the occasion arises, you can work on each of the other obstacles. Remember, the purpose of this exercise is to attract the positive opposite, not the other way around. If you feel you are slipping, simply imagine that you are holding up a shield and immediately think... *"I am attracting the opposite of this obstacle now! My Inner*

Magician is here to help me and I am now a Magician Apprentice. I am strong and I believe in ME."

Step 8:

Be grateful for your experience. Thank the inner Magician within you. Use this space to write more about your experience.

Remember:

Attitude • Gratitude • Happiness • Joy

CONGRATULATIONS!

NOTES

PART IV

PUTTING IT ALL TOGETHER

By this time, you may have an idea as to the direction I have
been taking you. Out of my own experience, I have realized
how important it is to fully understand the process of creating an
intention.

Doing the *groundwork* – understanding what is needed for an
intention to work, understanding what the *obstacles* are that may
keep an intention from working – and finally the *process* itself.

It's time to reach for the stars.

Create your own Magic

Become a Magic of Intention Apprentice

See the life you want

Use the tools and voilá

M•A•G•I•C

O•F

I•N•T•E•N•T•I•O•N

Are you ready to grab your wand?

Now your are acting like the real Magician that you are!

WHAT DO YOU REALLY WANT?

CHAPTER 19

This entire book is about goals. Setting goals. Realistic goals.

*"**Goals** provide the energy source that powers our lives. One of the best ways we can get the most from the energy we have is to focus it. That is what **goals** can do for us; concentrate our energy."*

~ Denis Waitley,

Author of 'Seeds of Greatness'

Are you ready to concentrate and use your energy towards your goal, which is your destiny towards success?

I have been told that I can sing and I love to sing. Then I would hear someone say *"Your voice is great, but you need some training."* Nice try! I want to sing.

You know what I am doing now? I am working as a music therapist with children of special needs. This fall I will be working with the adults. Don't tell me I cannot sing – I CAN! Do I want to be a professional singer? No, not really. Most of the time I cannot remember the lyrics, but I still love to sing. So realistically, I see myself as a singer just for a select few. It is okay that I won't be a professional singer. Recognizing that I love to sing, knowing I will not be a professional singer, is a mark of success. Because I have made the choice – not someone else – is my mark of success.

So let's do a little digging into YOUR goals.

"When you get right down to the meaning of the word SUCCEED, you find it simply means follow through."

~ F. W. Nichol,
VP and General Manager, IBM

Do you really want to succeed in life? Great! Now it is time to make a list of the goals you want to achieve. Following through with what you said you want to do is an indication that you are on the road to success!

"When it comes to riches, do you measure it in money or memories?"

~ Patricia Fripp,

Motivational Speaker, Author

"If the 20th century taught us anything, it is to be cautious about the word impossible."

~ Charles Platt,

Author & Contributor to 'Wired Magazine'

"Whatever you can do, or dream you can, begin it! Boldness has genius, power, and magic in it."

~ Goethe,

German Playwright

Give yourself credit. You can change any situation by waving your wand. Let go of the negative "I can't" – believe you can and see it happen NOW!

Get excited!

YOUR WORDS ARE YOUR WANDS!

Throw them around – see the Magic sparkle!

Stay focused

Be Proactive

Dare to Dream

Be Bold

Feel Your Personal Power

Visualize

Believe in Yourself

———————

*"Our **goals** can only be reached through a vehicle of a plan, in which we must fervently believe, and upon which we must vigorously act. There is no other route to success."*

~ Pablo Picasso,

Famed Spanish Artist

GOALS:

- Use concentrated energy

- Strategize

- Follow through

- Believe that everything and anything is possible

- Begin working on it NOW!

- Add determination to the magical ingredients

Determination will help you along the journey towards your ultimate goal and will break down obstacles which were discussed in Part III.

"It's the constant and determined effort that breaks down all resistance and sweeps away all obstacles."

~ Claude M. Bristol

Author, 'The Magic of Believing'

Exercise: **Goals** *(Write your experience)*

What do you want to accomplish in this lifetime? Make a list of all the goals/accomplishments you want to achieve. It can be as long or as short as you want it. Remember, goals change as you change.

Now, narrow it down to 20. (If you can't think of 20, that's ok. Just come back to this list sometime. Know that your goals change as you change.)

    1.

    2.

    3.

    4.

    5.

    6.

    7.

8.

9.

10.

11.

12.

13.

14.

15.

16.

17.

18.

19.

20.

Narrow that list to the top 10

1.

2.

3.

4.

5.

6.

7.

8.

9.

10.

Narrow the list to the top 5 and stop!

1.

2.

3.

4.

5.

Take those five goals/desires and prioritize them.

Number 1 on my list is _____

_____

Can you visualize yourself achieving this goal?

(If you can't, grab another goal from the top five quickly.)

Forget why you chose the number one goal in your life – instead, ask yourself the following question: Can you get excited about this goal?

How do you feel about telling others of your goal?

What is the 1st step you are going to take NOW?

INTUITION and COINCIDENCE

Chapter 20

Have you ever had a hunch and not followed it? Were you thinking about someone and they *happen* to call at that moment?

Intuition

Intuition can be thought of as a gut feeling or a hunch or simply a knowing.

---

*"**Intuition** is knowing what you know without knowing how you know it."*

~ **Cherlene Belitz, et al**

Author, 'The Power of Flow'

I do not know how many times I have had a "knowing" about something, just out of the blue. My husband finds it uncanny how I know about things without prior conscious evidence. I have noticed my intuition has become stronger the older I become. Perhaps this is a part of the journey through life. It's about *paying attention* and being connected or giving 'speaking permission' to that "wee little voice" inside.

I find that when I am in touch with my intuition, my creativity suddenly opens up. I take great pleasure when I know my intuition is working for me. In Chapter 2, I discussed the superconscious mind and how it can help give you insights. In trusting your intuition, you develop a sense of faith that you are on the right track. The "wee little voice" that is speaking to you is guiding you toward the goals you desire.

"The most beautiful thing we can experience is the mysterious."

~ Albert Einstein,
Physicist and Nobel Laureate

We already know that life is a mystery, so is our intuition. We cannot explain it but it's there to help us reach our goals, our hearts desire and our destiny. So why not be in touch with the gift that is within you? It is like having an on-call helper twenty-four hours a day.

Being in touch with your intuition requires a leap of faith.

Self-doubt, which was discussed in Chapter 10, can impede your progress and shut the door to your intuition.

———————

"Adventures don't begin until you get into the forest. The first step is an act of faith."

~ Mickey Hart,

Grateful Dead Drummer

While working on this book, I have had to open myself up to my intuition because this is my first publication. I had no idea how to write a book. The little voice inside of me just kept saying, "You can do it." I am listening.

———————

"Trust that still, small voice that says 'This might work' and I'll try it.'"

~ Diane Mariechild,

American Author

There are times when I feel as if my intuition has shut down. In reality, it doesn't… because it can't. This is your on-call helper that is right there waiting for you to pay attention. When I feel "out of touch" then I am not paying attention.

How do we know if "the message" is correct for us? There have been times when I felt that I was wrong, that my gut feeling made a mistake. And then I question my ability to "listen" to the wee voice inside. When the message is "wrong" that means I am out of touch. Intuition is never wrong. What is wrong is my interpretation.

––––––––––

"Do not fear mistakes – there are none."

~ Miles Davis,

American Trumpeter and Bandleader

Everything we do is an experience in life.

For example I was recently looking for a friend's house. I couldn't find it and I thought to myself "where is it?" I became impatient as I was supposed to have been there at a particular time. If I had been listening closely to my intuition, I would have known where to go. But, my impatience "blocked" the message that had the directions, so I just drove around in circles. Luckily I had my cell phone and called to get exact directions, which is what I should have done in the first place! I became frustrated with myself, which meant I was using negative energy that always blocks intuition.

When I am not in touch with my intuition, I feel a sense of loss … as if I lost my best friend. It's hard to explain unless you have experienced the same feeling. In order to be open to your intuition, you must be willing to listen to the little voice inside. When I get an intuitive "hit" I get excited about what just happened. This excitement and acknowledgement actually encourages my intuition to 'speak to me' because it 'knows' that I am listening – my radar is working.

---

*"....we need to be willing to let our **intuition** guide us, and be willing to follow that guidance directly and fearlessly."*

~ Shakti Gawain,

Motivational Author/International Speaker

How do you really know you are in touch with your intuition? According to France E. Vaughn in *Awakening Intuition*, there are four levels: Physical (gut feelings, headaches, neck pains); Emotional (sudden shift in ones mood); Mental (sudden brainstorming) and Spiritual (mystical experience).

What levels have you experienced?

We all are capable of experiencing our intuition, some more than others. Believe me when I say it is fun to be in touch. I feel ALIVE!

The following pages will have an exercise on Intuition. Have fun with it!

Most exercises, meditations, and visualizations,

will include my experiences for you to read as an example.

Remember, we are not alike and your experience

will be different from mine.

Exercise: **Intuition** *(Write your experience)*

This is the fun part of my book. I hope you are learning a lot about yourself... I certainly have learned a lot just in the writing. If you have some nice meditative music, go ahead and put that on. We're going to spend a little time getting in touch with your intuition. The best way to do this is to relax in a safe and comfortable place. Now think about the last time you were in touch with your intuition.

What was happening?

Was there a message?

Now, as you are relaxing ask a question – it can be a simple one, if you'd like. What is your question?

Sit quietly and let the answer come to you. If you do not receive an answer quickly, trust that you will. Sometimes answers come to me through a song on the radio, or something that someone has said. Let go of the question and simply trust that you will have an answer. Write down your experience.

Exercise: **Intuition** *(Sharing my experience)*

My Question is:

How do I market my Magic of Intention Motivational Cards?

The Answer is:

Let go of fear of failure. Re-read Susan Jeffer's book "Feel the Fear and Do It Anyway."

Believe in what I am doing – everyone else loves these motivational cards! I use them everyday – has made a huge difference in my life so why not share that with others and not be shy?

Get out of my office and start doing some networking. Let people know what I am doing.

Attract the perfect PR person who is in alignment with my works and understands them.

My Experience was

I feel positive and have a Can Do attitude!

I feel like I am on the right track.

I feel lighter.

Coincidence

From my own experiences, whenever I have a coincidental "event" I know I am in touch with my Intuition and that another clue as to what I am supposed to do just happened.

When a coincidence occurs, it can be a message about:

1) A memory of something from the past that needs to be looked at;

2) a person trying to contact me or tell me something;

3) I am on the right track. A clue to the next step;

4) a caution to be careful;

5) a spiritual awakening; or

6) a solution to a problem.

We experience coincidences everyday of our lives. The fun part is to recognize, acknowledge, and sort out what the meaning of the message is.

"If you do something once, people will call it an accident. If you do it twice, they call it a coincidence. But do it a third time and you've just proven a natural law. "

~ Grace Murray Hopper,

Pioneer Computer Scientist

A few months ago, I was at a winery where my husband and I are members. We were attending a picnic that was being offered by the owners in honor of the members.

There was a young man at our table who began talking about his Sunday music experience in Westchester County. He was working with children of special needs. Since I am working on my Ph.D. in Expressive Arts Therapy, I asked him if I could observe what he was doing. I explained the reason why and then enjoyed the rest of the day.

Apparently, my enthusiasm impressed him so much that within a few weeks I received a call stating that he had recommended me to take his place as he was leaving the organization. To make a long story short, I was hired for the two-hour sessions with the children. The Director was so impressed with my ideas that he is now allowing me to design my own program. In the Fall I will be working with the adults of special needs.

I never thought I would be working on a part-time basis at the Northern Westchester Center for the Arts, much less working with the Children of Special Needs. I do not have a background in this field, but do have a strong sense of the value that music can offer these children. The Spring session was a wonderful opportunity and now I am looking forward to more experiences. Plus, I am able to receive credit in my school program. It's a win-win situation, but if I had not been at the winery and met Reggie Bennett (the future American Idol and World Renown Singer of Musicals and Popular music – Outstanding Singer of the Year!) this would not have happened.

One small event led to a significant experience that not only opened my heart and mind to this group of children, but also moved me forward with my class experience. I consider this to be a wonderful blessing for me as well as a powerful 'coincidental' event.

Here's one more story, which is for all of you single people. I had been divorced for 20 years. Never did I think I would be divorced for such a long period of time. Eventually, I was resigned to being single. I was working on completing my under graduate degree, my children were almost grown, I had a fulfilling job, and life was good as a single person.

I was living in Austin, Texas at the time and would occasionally fly to England for business reasons. I had flown many times before, and I always dressed comfortably (jeans and tennis shoes). The trip that changed my life was about to start as I boarded the plane to England. I grabbed the window seat and made myself comfortable. Then a well-suited businessman came up to me and said I was in his seat. Naturally, I was going to move, but he said, "Never mind." He sat down next to me, being quite 'professional'.

Now, I'm a very outgoing person, so I began to talk to this stuffy businessman, but he would have nothing to do with me. He wanted to work and so I let him. Besides, I had things to work on as well. Then the meal came which opened the opportunity for some conversation. We began chatting – and we didn't stop for the rest of the trip (he was getting off at Atlanta and flying to his home in New York).

From that 'chance' encounter, we dated for over four years and have been married for three. I believe this was the most significant event I have ever had and the happiest. Ladies and Gentlemen, you never know when you are going to meet that special person. My suggestion is to be open to ALL possibilities.

I am sure you have plenty of stories to tell. I invite you to send me those stories as I will read each one with enthusiasm. Intuition and Coincidence act like a bank – series of checks and balances. How do you know if your intuition is correct? If you should follow your hunch? Look around you for the coincidental "ah-ha's" in your life, and don't expect the answer to always be obvious. You may receive answers in the form of a dream, a song, a picture, a wrong phone call, etc. That is what is fun about being in The Flow of life.

There are wonderful books on this subject. Go to the bookstore and randomly pick one or two or more. You will know which book you are supposed to read. Purchase a journal and keep track of your intuitive hunches and your coincidental events. I do this all the time. The more I acknowledge and write down the events, the hunches, the "ah-ha" moments, the more often they work. Magic Happens!

Recently, a ten year old girl was on the same flight with me and she said to me….about flying.

"Sometimes I wish I could fly to Heaven, but I think the plane would get tired."

~ Anon.

The innocence of this lovely, young child touched my heart and reminded me to be grateful for whatever comes my way. What was the message besides being grateful? Perhaps it was to take a leap of faith, to trust, to be enthusiastic about life!

I invite you to remember the coincidental events in your life and to realize that there is a message with each event. The following pages have an exercise on coincidences to help you better understand your journey in this area of living and to bring MORE MAGIC into your life.

"Chance is always powerful. Let your book be always cast; in the pool where you least expect it, there will be a fish."

~ Publius Ovidius Naso (Ovid),

Roman Poet

"Did you ever observe to whom the accidents happen? Chance favors only the prepared mind."

~ Louis Pasteur, *Microbiologist*
Discovered the cure for rabies

Most exercises, meditations, and visualizations,
will include my experiences for you to read as an example.
Remember, we are not alike and your experience
will be different from mine.

Exercise: **Coincidences** *(Write your experience)*
Write down every coincidental event you can recall happened to you in the last few years. If you need more space, grab some of your own paper. This is the time to reflect.

How did each event affect your life? (Remember some events are funny and are meant to remind you that you need to add humor into your life.)

Write down every coincidental event you can recall happened to you in the last few years'. If you need more space, grab some of your own paper. This is the time to reflect.

1) *Meeting my husband on the plane*

2) *Meeting my new friend in the little post office*

3) *Being at Ben Marl, the local winery, at the right time*

4) *Turning on TV and seeing a movie that reconfirmed my belief in Angels and that Angels are helping me through this process.*

5) *Meeting Sonia Penk, a wonderful German lady, who told me what her mother always said: "Remember the good advice you have given that day by wearing one earring."*

6) *Driving to another town, wondering about my life. I suddenly decided to put on a CD about Angels. I then looked up and saw a beautiful white dove flying over a parking lot. I knew then that I was being helped.*

7) *Calling a friend who needed some kind words at that particular moment.*

8) *Warning my husband that someone in his family could have some problems, only to find out that it was true the next day.*

How did each event affect your life? (Remember some events are funny and are meant to remind you that you need to add humor into your life.)

1) *I am now married to the man I met on the plane.*

2) *My new friend and I have become very close just when I was feeling lonely in the little town I live in.*

3) *Meeting Reggie had a profound impact on my life. Not only am I working with Children of Special Needs, I am no longer afraid to be around those who are not like me. I am about to see the beauty and wonderment that each offers.*

4) *I cried when the movie ended – they were tears of joy as I knew the Angels were with me.*

5) *Sonia is an amazing person. She is not only from my homeland, she is full of wisdom and inspiration. What a gift!*

6) *I was listening to the music from the TV show "Touched By An Angel" when that happened. I was thrilled!*

7) *My friend, Judy, has been distraught because another friend of ours is terminally ill and not wanting to live. Judy needed me to talk to her at the moment I called.*

8) *This did happen, unfortunately, and my husband was in awe that I had the ability, or sense, that something negative was coming to him quickly.*

FOCUS AGAIN

Chapter 21

In Chapter 7, I wrote about being focused. I am mentioning this again because focusing is one of the most important keys to your success.

Remember, you will not always be able to work on your goal, but consciously thinking about it and planning it in your mind will keep you focused.

Most of you have jobs and families to take care of, so you may only be able to spend a few evenings a week on your goal. That's fine. No one is going to test you. This is between you and you.

Focus is also a way of holding yourself accountable for what you have said. You said you want a degree in Biogenetics. Great.

You've told a few people your goal. Great. And now you have to "put up or shut up."

You're clear about what you want, you are willing to focus which holds you accountable, you are ready for the Magic to happen and then what?

I cannot emphasize enough how important it is to focus. This does not mean that you have to obsess. Obsessing is another block to your success and does not serve you well.

———————

"Act the part, and you will become the part."

~ William James,

American Philosopher

This means being in alignment with your heart's desire, moving forward, researching whatever you need, gathering the tools that will help you focus, and harnessing the MAGIC OF INTENTION .

As a reminder, please do not focus on what you have not completed, have not done. Focus on what you HAVE accomplished. Each time you accomplish one step, it's one less step you have to worry about.

"Aim at the sun and you may not reach it; but your arrow will fly far higher than if you had aimed at an object on a level with yourself."

~ F. Hawes

Author

Let the word FOCUS be your mantra and know that accountability is tagging along.

FOCUS • FOCUS • FOCUS

REINFORCEMENTS

Chapter 22

S oon, we will work on the specific technique. In the meantime, Part IV is a quick review of what Magical "tools" you need to write or say to create an intention. This chapter is about creating an environment that reminds you of your intention. These are the reinforcements of life.

Reinforcements

There are several ways we can reinforce our statements so that the subconscious mind BELIEVES that you are serious.

1) **Repetition** – take an intention and say or write it everyday until you feel that you do not need to do this any more

2) **Put your intention on a "sticky note"** and have it close by so you can glance at it often. For example, I will put one on my computer every morning. It may be the same one or a different one.

3) Develop a **support group** that believes in what you are doing. Do not, I repeat, do not invite those who will not or cannot emotionally support your goal. Some family members may not support you. What you may want to do is not talk about your goal in their presence. Have a telephone buddy close by when you are getting a little anxious or depressed that things are not happening fast enough; you can also share your achievements with them.

4) **Exercise gratitude.** This is my jingle – it's fun:

Attitude/Gratitude/Happiness/Joy

5) **Surround yourself with reminders of your goal.** I want to write an inspirational book so I have surrounded myself with books that inspire me. My little office is filled almost wall-to-wall with inspirational books.

6) **Journal writing.** This is a very important ritual! Keep a journal and write in it every morning and every evening. Write your thoughts, hopes, dreams, and frustrations, whatever. Always start your journal entry with an intention statement. I do this faithfully. Everything I am saying about reinforcing your intention – I do myself as well.

7) **Get into a Magic of Intention Circle** – Information about this will be on my website (http://www.magicofintention. com)

8) **Purchase a set of Magic of Intention Motivational cards** – and use them everyday. Some cards may not apply to your situation, so simply adjust the statement to fit you.

WORDS ARE YOUR WANDS

Chapter 23

**It is important to
be clear about your goal, and
be clear about your statement.**

---

*"Man's **word** is his **wand** filled with magic and power!"*

~ **Florence Scovel Schinn,**

Spirituality Author

In Chapter 2, I discussed a little about the power of your words. For example, if you use the phrase "I am sick of this job." Guess what, you may just get sick and lose your job. That is why you need to be very, very clear about your goal and the wording of your intention.

"People who believe things can't be done will go out and prove they are 'right'.

~ **Dr. Robert Anthony,**
Author of 'Think Again'

The following is a great example of the misuse of wording. Saying words like "I *can't*...it will be *impossible*...I won't be in control" is clearly self-defeating.

Don't be a slave of your words, be in control of your words. Swirl that wand around for YOUR benefit. There is Magic in your words, use them wisely and you won't lose the Magic.

Misuse of your words will only cause you distress, ill health, insecurity, in action, blame of others, etc.

Which do you choose?

"Life is a mirror; it reflects back whatever image we present to it."

~ **Dr. Robert Anthony,**
Author of 'Think On'

Your words are mirror images of who you are. If you say "I hate" – then look in the mirror and ask yourself, "whom or what do I really hate?"

"The Self exists both inside and outside the physical body, just as an image exists inside and outside the mirror."

~ Ashtavakra Gita,

Hindu Scripture

Do you see how this works?

Take some time to check out the words you use on a daily basis. There is always room for improvement. Are you ready to do some "house cleaning?"

The next chapter will contains a check list that will help you stay on track so you can achieve that which you would like to achieve. Look at the check list often and see where you may need some improvements, which ones you've accomplished and how well you've held yourself accountable. Remember, this is not a test – it is simply a way to gauge where you have improved and where you may need some improvement.

"Stop thinking and talking about it and there is nothing you will not be able to know."

~ Zen Paradigm

CHECK LIST

Chapter 24

I have included a checklist to help you clarify your goals and your actions before writing or saying a Magic of Intention statement. This checklist will include the obstacles.

Do you *BELIEVE* in your goal?

Are you *CLEAR* about your intention? Is there any doubt?

Is there *PURPOSE* behind your intention?

Are you ready to *EXPECT* the best *FOR YOURSELF*?

Do you have *INTEGRITY* for yourself and others?

Do you have the *COURAGE* to step out of the box?

Do you *BELIEVE* in your intention?

Do you *BELIEVE* in yourself?

Are you ready to *TAKE CHARGE* of your life?

Can you *VISUALIZE* yourself achieving your goal?

Can you *VISUALIZE* yourself one week after achieving your goal?

Can you *VISUALIZE* yourself one month later?

Can you *VISUALIZE* yourself one year later?

Can you *VISUALIZE* yourself five years later?

Are you 100% *FOCUSED* on your intention?

Are you ready to hold yourself *ACCOUNTABLE*?

Can you act "as if" it has *ALREADY HAPPENED*?

Have you released *SELF-DOUBT*?

Do you *TRUST* yourself?

Are you still *RESENTFUL*?

Have you let go of *RESISTANCE TO CHANGE*?

Are you ready to *STOP LOOKING BACK*?

Do you fully understand *KARMA*?

Are you ready to be *POSITIVE*?

Have you *LISTENED* to your *INTUITION* today?

What *COINCIDENTAL* events happened today?

Do you D*ARE TO BE YOU*?

Are you in touch with your *AUTHENTIC SELF*?

Have you set *BOUNDARIES* in order to reach your goals?

Have you *FORGIVEN* yourself as well as others?

Do you have a *SUPPORT GROUP*?

Can you *LAUGH*?

Are you ready to let go of your *FEARS AND WORRIES?*

Are you *JOURNALING?*

Are you paying close attention to your *WORDS?*

Are you *MEDITATING* everyday?

Are you *EXERCISING AND EATING* healthfully?

Are you *PAYING ATTENTION* to life?

Are you ready to be in the *PRESENT MOMENT?*

Do you really want to be *SUCCESSFUL?*

Are you ready to be in touch with your *SPIRITUAL SIDE?*

Are you reprogramming your *SUBCONSCIOUS MIND* so it will work for you?

Can you *LOVE YOURSELF* and others?

Are you willing to *SEE THE FREE SPIRIT* in you?

Are you open to the *CREATIVE SIDE OF YOU?*

Have you let go of those things that are *HOLDING* you back?

ADD TO YOUR CHECK LIST

And more......

TECHNIQUE

Chapter 25

If you've read all the chapters and completed the checklist, you are now ready for the technique.

Start with the words "I intend":

You and no one else is doing the intending

Next – use the words "that I":

This means that **YOU** *are holding* <u>*yourself*</u> *accountable (no one else).* This "tells" your subconscious mind that **YOU MEAN BUSINESS**! It also allows the subconscious mind to accept your *New Programming.*

Next – use an action verb in the statement:

This implies that you are taking action and it is happening right away.

Finally – add the word NOW:

Somewhere in the statement I always add the word NOW to create an environment of excitement and believability. Remember earlier I talked about Acting As If It Is Happening NOW! The "It" is your intention.

This is what the intention may look like:

I intend that I am *accepting* my success **NOW!**

I intend that I am *believing* in me *NOW*!

Even though your intention may be something that will happen in the near future, it is important to put the energy in the present. If you want your intention to happen faster – and not doubt what you are intending – then make it in the present.

Now it's your turn. Words like "I hope" and "I will" are implying that something is going to happen in the future. Stay away from those words as I am sure you want your intention to happen NOW! *So think and remember to act as if it has already happened.* And drop the "I don't believe this attitude." Part V will contain samples from A-Z.

THE MAGIC WORKS WHEN YOU BELIEVE.
GRAB THE WAND OF SUCCESS
N O W!
AND START CREATING A BETTER LIFE.

Your New Mantra:

I intend that I am • I intend that I am

The last section of this book will contain samples of intentions from A-Z. With each section, there will be space for you to make

203

up your own. Thank you for joining me in this journey. Please let me know what your journey is once you have started reading this book.

Namasté, Karin

PART V

SAMPLE INTENTION
A-Z

A_____

ABANDON

I intend that I am **NOW** *abandoning* thoughts of resentment and anger, as they no longer serve me.

ABUNDANCE

I intend that I attract *abundance* into my life by continually being prepared for new opportunities **NOW**!

ABUSE

I intend that I am no longer abusing my body with unhealthy substances NOW! I am NOW protecting my body by _____

_____

ACCEPT

I intend that I **NOW** *accept* who I am. I am looking in the mirror and see the Miracle I am **NOW**!

ACCOUNTABLE

I intend that I am holding myself accountable for my actions NOW! These actions are _____

_____

Now it is your turn with the A's

I intend that I

_____

_____

I intend that I

_____

_____

I intend that I

_____

_____

I intend that I

_____

_____

I intend that I

_____

_____

I intend that I

_____

_____

I intend that I

_____

_____

B_____

BACKGROUND

I intend that I am accepting my childhood *background* as a gift and using that gift to help others **NOW**!

BALLOON

I intend that I am inflating a *balloon,* putting all my troubles in it, and letting them go **NOW**! I am free of troubles **NOW**!

BEAR HUG

I intend that I am giving myself a *bear hug* for all the achievements I have made throughout my lifetime **NOW**!

BECOME

I intend that I am *becoming* the person I want to be **NOW**!

BEHAVIOR

I intend that I am recognizing unhealthy *behavior* patterns and am making adjustments **NOW**!

BELIEF

I intend that I am changing my *belief* system towards a more positive outlook **NOW**!

Now it is your turn with the B's

I intend that I

_____

_____

I intend that I

_____

_____

I intend that I

_____

_____

I intend that I

_____

_____

I intend that I

_____

_____

I intend that I

_____

_____

I intend that I

_____

_____

C_____

CALCIUM

I intend that I am taking responsibility for the strength of my bones by taking *calcium* on a regular basis **NOW**!

CANCER

I intend that I see my *cancer* as an opportunity for personal growth and that I am learning as much as I need to learn **NOW**!

CANVASS

I intend that I paint the *canvas* of my life with zest and meaning **NOW**!

COMPLETION

I intend that I am grateful for this new day and that it is a perfect day for *completion* of all my projects **NOW**!

CONDEMNING

I intend that I am no longer *condemning* people who have hurt me. I am **NOW** blessing those people and releasing them to their highest good.

Now it is your turn with the C's

I intend that I

_____

_____

I intend that I

_____

_____

I intend that I

_____

_____

I intend that I

_____

_____

I intend that I

_____

_____

I intend that I

_____

_____

I intend that I

_____

_____

D_____

DASH

I intend that I *dash* away all negative thoughts that are harmful to me **NOW**!

DEAL

I intend that I am dealing with my present situation and handling it NOW! The situation I am NOW dealing with is _____

_____.

DEBT

I intend that I am *debt-free* by making conscious changes in my life **NOW**!

DECEITFUL

I intend that I am attracting honest people rather than *deceitful* people into my life **NOW**!

DECISION

I intend that I am making positive decisions that will impact my life NOW! These decisions are _____

_____.

Now it is your turn with the D's

I intend that I

_____

_____

I intend that I

_____

_____

I intend that I

_____

_____

I intend that I

_____

_____

I intend that I

_____

_____

I intend that I

_____

_____

I intend that I

_____

_____

E_____

EARTH

I intend that I am honoring Mother Earth and am taking care of
Her **NOW!** I am honoring Mother Earth by _____

_____

_____

EDUCATION

I intend that I am receiving an *education* that will enhance my
future **NOW!**

EFFECTIVE

I intend that I am being an *effective* speaker **NOW!**

EFFORTLESSLY

I intend that I am *effortlessly* attracting prosperous clients
NOW!

ENDLESS

I intend that I am accepting that *endless* good is coming to me in
endless ways **NOW!**

Now it is your turn with the E's

I intend that I

_____

_____

I intend that I

_____

_____

I intend that I

_____

_____

I intend that I

_____

_____

I intend that I

_____

_____

I intend that I

_____

_____

I intend that I

_____

_____

F_____

FAILURES

I intend that I am experiencing any *failures* I encounter as simply opportunities to learn and grow mentally, spiritually, and physically **NOW**!

FAITH

I intend that I am filled with *faith* and trust that my heart's desire is **NOW** coming to fruition in a most miraculous way!

FATIGUED

I intend that I am listening to my body when I am feeling fatigued! My fatigue is caused by _____ _____ and I am taking care of it NOW!

FORGIVENESS

I intend that I am NOW open to forgiveness and choose to neutralize a situation that has been unpleasant for me. I am NOW forgiving _____ _____

Now it is your turn with the F's

I intend that I

_____

_____

I intend that I

_____

_____

I intend that I

_____

_____

I intend that I

_____

_____

I intend that I

_____

_____

I intend that I

_____

_____

I intend that I

_____

_____

G_____

GAINFULLY

I intend that I am *gainfully* employed in the most empowering and life-enhancing way **NOW!**

GARBAGE

I intend that I am NOW releasing ALL emotional garbage that has kept me in a state of confusion. That emotional garbage was

_____

_____

GENERATING

I intend that I am generating enthusiasm for the work that I am doing NOW! That work is _____

_____

GENIUS

I intend that I am letting the *genius* within me come out and clearly help me see the perfect plan for me **NOW!**

GIVING

I intend that I am opening up the way to receiving by *giving* **NOW!** The more I give, the more I receive. (Attitude/Gratitude/ Happiness/Joy)

Now it is your turn with the G's

I intend that I

_____

_____

I intend that I

_____

_____

I intend that I

_____

_____

I intend that I

_____

_____

I intend that I

_____

_____

I intend that I

_____

_____

I intend that I

_____

_____

H_____

HABITS

I intend that I am changing my habits to fit the new me NOW!

The habits I am changing are _____

_____

HARMONY

I intend that I am in perfect *harmony* with life and am dancing with the music of life **NOW!**

HEAL

I intend that I *heal* my heart through the assistance of a loving support group, a life coach, or counselor **NOW!**

HIRED

I intend that I am NOW being *hired* in a dream position at a company of my choice **NOW!**

HOUSE

I intend that I am giving thanks for the *house,* which is mine by divine right **NOW!**

Now it is your turn with the H's

I intend that I

_____

_____

I intend that I

_____

_____

I intend that I

_____

_____

I intend that I

_____

_____

I intend that I

_____

_____

I intend that I

_____

_____

I intend that I

_____

_____

I_____

IDEAL

I intend that I am seeking my ideal relationship NOW! My ideal

relationship is _____

_____

IDENTIFY

I intend that I freely identify with the person I want to be NOW!

That person is _____

_____

IMBALANCES

I intend that I am understanding past imbalances of my life and

am dealing with them NOW! The first balancing step is _____

_____

IMPOSSIBLE

I intend that I am replacing the word *impossible* with possible

NOW!

INSPIRATION

I intend that I am open to direct *inspiration* and am making the

correct decisions in my life **NOW!**

Now it is your turn with the I's

I intend that I

_____

_____

I intend that I

_____

_____

I intend that I

_____

_____

I intend that I

_____

_____

I intend that I

_____

_____

I intend that I

_____

_____

I intend that I

_____

_____

J

JAZZING

I intend that I am *jazzing* up my wardrobe **NOW!**

JEOPARDIZE

I intend that I am no longer *jeopardizing* of my happiness by remaining stuck in my old patterns **NOW!**

JEWEL

I intend that I am acknowledging the jewel of a relationship that I have NOW! These relationship is _____

JOBLESSNESS

I intend that I am no longer accepting my *joblessness* and am actively seeking employment **NOW!**

JOGGING

I intend that I am including *jogging* as an integrated part of my exercise program **NOW!** I am committed to *jogging* _____ miles per day.

Now it is your turn with the J's

I intend that I

_____

_____

I intend that I

_____

_____

I intend that I

_____

_____

I intend that I

_____

_____

I intend that I

_____

_____

I intend that I

_____

_____

I intend that I

_____

_____

K_____

KALEIDOSCOPE

I intend that I am looking through the *kaleidoscope* of my life and am seeing the beauty and Divine complexity of my journey **NOW**!

KEY

I intend that I am holding the *key* to my success **NOW**! I am turning the *key* to success **NOW**!

KEYNOTE

I intend that I am a *keynote* speaker **NOW**! My topic is both motivational and inspiring.

KICKING UP

I intend that I am kicking up my heels and having fun NOW! My fun is _____

KINDNESS

I intend that I am showing kindness to those in need NOW! The way I am showing kindness is by _____

_____

_____.

Now it is your turn with the K's

I intend that I

_____

_____

I intend that I

_____

_____

I intend that I

_____

_____

I intend that I

_____

_____

I intend that I

_____

_____

I intend that I

_____

_____

I intend that I

_____

_____

L_____

LADDER

I intend that I am climbing the *ladder* of success by not stepping on others **NOW**!

LANGUAGE

I intend that I am learning a language that I have always wanted to learn NOW! That language is _____

_____

LAUGHTER

I intend that I am bringing more laughter into my life. I am NOW laughing about _____

LEADING

I intend that I am leading the kind of life I have always wanted to lead NOW! That life is _____

_____

LIMITING

I intend that I am not *limiting* my abundance by *limiting* my vision and trust. My vision and trust are clear **NOW** and forever more!

Now it is your turn with the L's

I intend that I

_____

_____

I intend that I

_____

_____

I intend that I

_____

_____

I intend that I

_____

_____

I intend that I

_____

_____

I intend that I

_____

_____

I intend that I

_____

_____

M_____

MAGIC

I intend that I am inviting the *magic* into my life and this magic is happening **NOW**!

MAGNET

I intend that I am a *magnet* for all good things to happen **NOW**!

MANAGING

I intend that I am *managing* my daily activities so that I have time to enjoy my life **NOW**!

MAGICAL

I intend that I am experiencing *magical* works in a *magical* way **NOW**!

MONEY

I intend that I am seeing *money* flowing naturally and effortlessly as it circulates through my life **NOW**!

Now it is your turn with the M's

I intend that I

_____

_____

I intend that I

_____

_____

I intend that I

_____

_____

I intend that I

_____

_____

I intend that I

_____

_____

I intend that I

_____

_____

I intend that I

_____

_____

N_____

NARRATE

I intend that I am narrating my life the way I want it to be NOW!

The story of ME will be filled with _____

_____

NEARSIGHTED

I intend that I am seeing my world clearly through new and improved vision by eliminating my *nearsighted* views of it **NOW**!

NOISE

I intend that I am making loud *noises* of good cheer to reach all of mankind **NOW**!

NON-RESISTANCE

I intend that I am practicing *non-resistance* whenever I feel resentment towards someone. I bless that person, send them on their way, and waste no energy on the emotion of resentment **NOW**!

Now it is your turn with the N's

I intend that I

_____

_____

I intend that I

_____

_____

I intend that I

_____

_____

I intend that I

_____

_____

I intend that I

_____

_____

I intend that I

_____

_____

I intend that I

_____

_____

O_____

OBSTACLES

I intend that I am tearing down all *obstacles* towards my good. The walls of obstacles no longer exist and I am free to achieve my heart's desire **NOW!**

OCCUPATION

I intend that I am attracting an *occupation* of my choice **NOW!**

OCEAN

I intend that I am experiencing the sounds of the *ocean,* which bring tranquility into my life **NOW!**

ODDS AND ENDS

I intend that I am letting go of any *odds and ends* of my life that no longer fit the lifestyle of my choice **NOW!**

OPPORTUNITIES

I intend that I am open to new opportunities for a new beginning NOW!   Those opportunities are _____

_____

Now it is your turn with the O's

I intend that I

_____

_____

I intend that I

_____

_____

I intend that I

_____

_____

I intend that I

_____

_____

I intend that I

_____

_____

I intend that I

_____

_____

I intend that I

_____

_____

P_____

PEACE

I intend that I am at *peace* with myself and with the world around me **NOW**!

PERFECT PLAN

I intend that, in every moment, I am designing the *perfect plan* that includes health, abundance, love and creativity **NOW**!

PLENTY

I intend that I am filled with Divine Love and that I receive *plenty* of what it is that I most need **NOW**!

POWER

I intend that I am allowing the *power* within me to move mountains of love, success, peace, joy and gratitude **NOW**!

PROSPERITY

I intend that I am accepting *prosperity* in all areas of my life and in perfect ways **NOW**!

Now it is your turn with the P's

I intend that I

_____

_____

I intend that I

_____

_____

I intend that I

_____

_____

I intend that I

_____

_____

I intend that I

_____

_____

I intend that I

_____

_____

I intend that I

_____

_____

R_____

REINCARNATION

I intend that I am entering my final *incarnation* as the cycle of life of Earth ends **NOW**!

RELEASE

I intend that I am *releasing* all fears and accepting avalanches of abundance in miraculous ways **NOW**!

RESENTMENT

I intend that I am casting out the burden of *resentment* and am **NOW** free to be loving, kind, balanced, and joyous.

RICH

I intend that I am thinking, feeling, and acting as if I am *rich* in every area of my life **NOW**! I know that everything is possible.

RHYTHM

I intend that I am in tune with the *rhythm* of life, which includes harmony and balance. This contributes to my success **NOW**!

Now it is your turn with the R's

I intend that I

_____

_____

I intend that I

_____

_____

I intend that I

_____

_____

I intend that I

_____

_____

I intend that I

_____

_____

I intend that I

_____

_____

I intend that I

_____

_____

S_____

SPENDING

I intend that I am **NOW** *spending* wisely and fearlessly with the knowledge that my supply is endless and immediate.

SIMPLE RULES

I intend that I am **NOW** incorporating into my daily life the *simple rules* of success, which are trust, non-resistance, fearlessness and love.

SORROW

I intend that I am replacing *sorrow* with joy and realizing the good that comes from it **NOW**!

SUCCESS

I intend that I am walking through doors to my *success* which have always been opened to me. All other doors that are not in my best interest will remain closed starting **NOW**!

SURPRISES

I intend that I am boldly accepting life's joyous *surprises'* as opportunities for a brighter future **NOW**!

Now it is your turn with the S's

I intend that I

_____

_____

I intend that I

_____

_____

I intend that I

_____

_____

I intend that I

_____

_____

I intend that I

_____

_____

I intend that I

_____

_____

I intend that I

_____

_____

T_____

TO-DO-LIST

I intend that I am incorporating a *to-do-list* into my daily life in order to achieve balance **NOW**!

TOO LATE

I intend that I am believing that it is never *too late* to receive the good fortune that I desire **NOW**!

TRAFFIC

I intend that I am seeing the *traffic* of opportunity, success, happiness and abundance running smoothly in my life **NOW**!

TRANQUILITY

I intend that I am filled with tranquility as I look out of my window and see the beauty of _____ **NOW**!

TRUTH

I intend that I am facing the *truth* of my fears by letting go of self-deception **NOW**! My personal *truth* is _____

_____

Now it is your turn with the T's

I intend that I

_____

_____

I intend that I

_____

_____

I intend that I

_____

_____

I intend that I

_____

_____

I intend that I

_____

_____

I intend that I

_____

_____

I intend that I

_____

_____

U_____

UNBROKEN

I intend that I am in the Flow as my success is growing steadily and in an *unbroken pace* **NOW**!

UNEXPECTED

I intend that I am **NOW** experiencing some *unexpected* events and am handling them well. Those unexpected events are _____

_____

UNRELIABLE

I intend that I am no longer *unreliable* as I hold myself accountable **NOW**!

UTOPIAN

I intend that I am researching the concept of a *utopian* society to understand how I can incorporate some of those ideals into my present life **NOW**!

U-TURN

I intend that I am understanding the reasons why I sometimes have to take u-turns while navigating my life's journey. Some of those u-turns are: _____

_____

Now it is your turn with the U's

I intend that I

_____

_____

I intend that I

_____

_____

I intend that I

_____

_____

I intend that I

_____

_____

I intend that I

_____

_____

I intend that I

_____

_____

I intend that I

_____

_____

V_____

VALUE

I intend that I am creating a personal *value* list in order to better understand who I am **NOW**!

VIRTUE

I intend that I am demonstrating the virtues that I define who I am NOW! Those virtues are _____

VIVID

I intend that I have a *vivid* imagination that lets me see the larger scheme of things **NOW**!

VOICE

I intend that I am listening to the *voice* of intuition and honoring what it is saying by trusting The Source **NOW**!

Now it is your turn with the V's

I intend that I

_____

_____

I intend that I

_____

_____

I intend that I

_____

_____

I intend that I

_____

_____

I intend that I

_____

_____

I intend that I

_____

_____

I intend that I

_____

_____

W_____

WALKING

I intend that I am boldly *walking* with a brisk, constant pace that is good for my health **NOW!**

WARRIOR

I intend that I am raising the wand and the *warrio*r within me is courageously moving towards my success **NOW!**

WHIRLWIND

I intend that I am enjoying the *whirlwind* of success **NOW!** While being successful I am remaining balanced and connected.

WISHING

I intend that I am clear about what it is that I am wishing for NOW! My greatest wish is _____ _____

_____

WORRY

I intend that I am sending all my *worries* to the Magician of *Worry* **NOW!** The Magician of *Worry* swirls the magical wand and changes *worry* into confidence **NOW!**

Now it is your turn with the W's

I intend that I

_____

_____

I intend that I

_____

_____

I intend that I

_____

_____

I intend that I

_____

_____

I intend that I

_____

_____

I intend that I

_____

_____

I intend that I

_____

_____

XYZ_____

X-Ray

I intend that I am taking a mental *x-ray* of my thoughts and am zapping all negative thoughts that are clear to me **NOW**!

YARDSTICK

I intend that I am using a yardstick to measure the quality of life I have now versus that in my past. This yardstick reveals

_____

YEAR

I intend that I am looking at each New *Year* as a New Me that is being reinvented **NOW**!

YESTERDAYS

I intend that I honor the important yesterdays of my life and release them by living in the present moments NOW! My yesterdays were _____

_____

ZEN

I intend that I am practicing *Zen* meditation **NOW**!

Now it is your turn with the X, Y, Z's

I intend that I

_____

_____

I intend that I

_____

_____

I intend that I

_____

_____

I intend that I

_____

_____

I intend that I

_____

_____

I intend that I

_____

_____

I intend that I

_____

_____

PEOPLE IN THE KNOW

Perry A~ *<PerryA@PerryA.com>*

Speaker, Author and World's Only Dessert Analyst

512-441-0335 Fax 512-441-0206

www.PerryA.com

Reggie Bennett *<bennett2g@aol.com>*

Teacher and Singer: Musicals, Operas, Actor, Popular Music

Lori Bonfitto <Lori.Bonfitto@AIG.com>

Writer, Performer

Plays written and produced in New York:

Spies in the Stacks; A Very Special 1Hour Georgie, and Groupies

Larry Czerwonka *<larry@buzztone.com>*

Works with numerous companies and government agencies to help foster better communication in the workplace and eliminate the need for meetings. Currently is creating a web site where people will be able to earn a happiness degree: (http://www.happinessu. org) which is expected to launch in the 4th quarter of 2004.

Dr. Stan Friedland <stanfree@optonline.net>

Author, Educator

"Play It Again Sam", Xlibris, publisher.

252

Dr. Barbara Becker Holstein *<Encself@aol.com>*

Positive Psychology and Happiness Coach

http://www.enchantedself.com

Roger King *<roger@soulatalkstories.com>*

Author, Counselor, Motivational Speaker

www.SoulTalkStories.com

Dee Saunders *<Mixedme372@aol.com>*

Nationally Certified Therapist/Counselor

Board Certified Expressive Therapist, Faculty member for NIET

Nancy Gay Smith <Tendrft@aol.com>

Freelance Writer/Professional Proof Reader

512-288-0639.

Joanne Susi, *<coachsusi@comcast.net>*

Professional Life Coach, Faculty member of Coach Training

Alliance (http://3pointcoaching.com/)

Chelle Thompson *<ChelleThompson@InspirationLine.com>*

Background in Philosophy, Motivational Speaking, Recovery Counseling, International Travel Writing and Theology www. InspirationLine.com

SUGGESTED READING

Co-Active Coaching by *Laura Whitworth*

Face the Fear and Do It Anyway, *Susan Jeffers*

Love the Miracle You Are by *Roger King*

Million Dollar Habits by *Brian Tracy*

Molecules of Emotion, by *Candace B. Pert, Ph.D.*

Radical Forgiveness by *Colin C. Tipping*

Recipes for Enchantment by *Dr. Barbara Becker Holstein*

Spiritual Marketing by *Joe Vitale*

Spontaneous Fulfillment of Desire by *Deepak Chopra, M.D.*

The Art of Possibility by *Rosamund Stone Zander and Benjamin Zander*

The Five People You Meet In Heaven by *Mitch Albom*

The Power of Flow by *Charlene Beltiz, et. al*

The Power of Full Engagement by *Jim Loehr, et al*

The Power of Intention by *Dr. Wayne Dyer*

The Saint, The Surfer, and The CEO by *Robin Sharma*

The Wisdom of Florence Scovel Shinn by *Florence Scovel Shinn*

Vibrating To Spirit, *Kathleen Tucci*

What Happy People Know by *Dan Baker, Ph.D.*

Your Heart's Desire by *Sonia Choquette, Ph.D.*

WEB SITES:

Roger King, *Author, Inspirational Speaker*

http://www.SoulTalkStories.com

Brian Tracy, *Author, Motivational Speaker*

http://www.BrianTtracy.com

Peter Shepherd. *Transformational Psychologist*

http://www.trans4mind.com

Joanne Susi, *Personal Life Coach, Mentor and Trainer*

http://www.3pointcoaching.com/

Chelle Thompson, *Editor, Writer, Spiritual Teacher*

http://www.InspirationOnLine.com

The Orphan Connection

http://www.OrphanConnect.com

Magic of Intention

http://www.MagicOfIntention.com

ProVoice Speakers Bureau

http://www.provoicespeakers.com/

Quotes:

http://www.brainyquote.com/

http://www.boardofwisdom.com/default.asp

http://www.motivational-inspirational-corner.com/

ABOUT THE AUTHOR

Karin has a degree in Psychology, is a Certified Creativity life Coach, the mother of three and Gran Mopsey to four children. She is married to a successful lawyer and is working towards her Ph.D. in Expressive Arts Therapy.

Karin is also the founder of The Orphan Connection (http:// www.orphanconnect.com) a non-profit organization which honors orphans that are making a difference in the lives of others. Karin invites you to write in inspirational orphan stories.

For more information on Karin Janin, speaking engagements, workshops or her Magic of Intention Life coaching, you can write her at:

Karin Janin

P.O. Box 607

Highland, NY 12528

Or visit her website at: www.KarinJanin.com

Made in the USA
Columbia, SC
25 September 2021